T0209522

A CRAGGY PEBBLE BECOMES A SMOOTH ROCK

A Study of Simon Peter and His Ministry

MARY ALYCE BAKER

WESTBOW
PRESS®
A DIVISION OF THOMAS NELSON
& ZONDERVAN

WestBow Press books may be ordered through booksellers or by contacting:

WestBow Press
A Division of Thomas Nelson & Zondervan
1663 Liberty Drive
Bloomington, IN 47403
www.westbowpress.com
844-714-3454

ISBN: 978-1-6642-6056-6 (sc)
ISBN: 978-1-6642-6055-9 (e)

Library of Congress Control Number: 2022904569

Print information available on the last page.

WestBow Press rev. date: 03/31/2022

CONTENTS

ABOUT THE AUTHOR

Mary Alyce Baker has been a follower of Christ for 45 years. She's devoted to the study and teaching of God's Word. Across the years, she has led Bible studies in homes, churches, and anywhere the Lord leads her. She and her husband, Don, have been married for 55 years, and make their home in Gulfport, Mississippi, where they serve in ministry at their church. They have two children and three grandchildren.

ACKNOWLEDGMENTS

Argile Smith, Ph.D.
Gary E. Blackwell, Ph.D.

Thank you for your wisdom, background, and knowledge of scripture, guidance, and direction in all aspects in the creation of this study of the Lord's great apostle and his accomplishments, in spite of his weaknesses.

Helen Dunn, Joan Middleton, and those who attended this study, both live and virtually. Your encouragement, your support, and most of all, your prayers have given me the desire and determination to take this study of Peter's life and ministry forward to share with others.

CHAPTER 1

Simon Peter Meets and Walks with Jesus

The Lord has been laying Simon Peter upon my heart for some time. Then one day, while walking in my neighborhood, I happened to look down at a neighbor's landscaping, and my attention was drawn to the array of rocks and stones that enhanced the bed. As I gazed down, the Holy Spirit brought my attention to three of them. One was small, rough, and craggy, the next was a little larger and smoother, while the third was smooth and attractive.

He then told me that these are images of Simon Peter. The first one represents the fisherman when Jesus gave him a new name and called him to follow Him. He not only saw his weaknesses and limitations, but He also saw the man, once smoothed out to become what He intended him to be, as "a rock of defense for Christ and a pillar in the temple of Christ."[1] Christ does not choose the prepared but chooses those He can equip. As we work through this great apostle's life and works, please look at your life. Are you a Simon or a Peter? Are you willing to let go and allow the Lord to work in your life to be the person He has a vision for you to be?

Jesus spoke more of Peter than any of the others, both in a positive and negative manner. Peter was discipled more than the others. He courageously reproved Jesus. He confessed and acknowledged Jesus more than the others as well as interfered with and tempted his Lord. Yet Jesus spoke praises and blessings to him more than the others; however, He also voiced strong words to him. Let us now walk through the life of this fisherman turned disciple to apostle to see what we can learn from him. Why? Because he was so much like you and me as we walk the path of growing in our faith and working for our Lord—our one and only Savior.

John the Baptist was preaching in the Jordan Valley while preparing the way for the coming of Christ and the need for repentance. He announced Jesus to those hearing as being the Lamb of God. Andrew, Peter's brother, heard him and went to find Peter. He then brought him to meet Jesus, declaring that the Messiah had been found (John 1:41). It was common for the Jewish people

---

[1] A. T. Robertson, *Epochs in the Life of Simon Peter* (Charles Scribner's Sons, 1935), 17.

to seek the Messiah. It is sad to see so many of God's people still searching and not allowing Jesus to fulfill the scriptures in their lives, which He did as Isaiah described perfectly in chapter 53.

John tells us he was a native of Bethsaida, which was on the shore of the Sea of Galilee, where Jesus often walked and talked with the people. His birth name was Simon Bar-Jona, with his last name meaning "son of John." His first name is also spelled Simeon and Symeon and means "listening." That is one of the definitions of a disciple: one who follows or is a student of someone. They listen and learn from the teacher, who will be Jesus, the Rabbi they would follow. When Jesus looked at Simon, He proclaimed that he was Simon and that he would now be addressed as Cephas (pronounced Kay-fas) (John 1:42), which means "a stone" (*Petros,* or Peter, means "the man of rock").

This may seem strange, but not in the eyes of the Lord. Why? As we shall see, this name vaguely fits him at the onset. You might say he was much more like a crag cut out of the side of a mountain, with sharp points jetting out of it; however, we will see these sharp points or crags smoothed into a beautiful, steadfast stone by the transformation of the hand of the Master, Who would recreate him into the stone selected by the builder to go forward and become the apostle as we know him today, through reading God's Word.

Peter is the visionary of churches throughout the world. We assume he was educated in a Jewish school and was able to converse in both Greek and Aramaic; however, he had no rabbinical training. He came from a family of fishermen. He and his brother, Andrew, worked with James and John, the sons of Zebedee. John stands out as he wrote the epistles of John and the great prophetic book of Revelation. Simon Peter had great friends to walk beside him as they followed Jesus together.

Peter would leave his childhood home and go to Capernaum, where he would reside with his wife and mother-in-law. His life was on the water, with a successful fishing business. We do not know his wife's name or if they had any children. We do know she went on mission trips with him (1 Corinthians 9:5).

Now let us walk down the path of Peter's life after meeting Jesus and receiving his new name, with a purpose that will be revealed as we cover his new life. Replace his name with yours, as you will see yourself in so many ways.

The next time he meets Jesus is recorded in Matthew 4:18, Mark 1:16–18, and Luke 5:1–11, when Jesus is gathering up those He chooses to be His disciples; the first four are fishermen. Jesus was walking along the Sea of Galilee and spotted Simon (Peter) and Andrew working with the nets on their boat. Jesus called out to them and asked them to follow Him, as He wanted to make them fishers of men (Mark 1:17). John Walvoord wrote that Jesus was calling them to be a part of His kingdom, and now He would begin to equip them to share His task. He was calling them to gather people from out of the sea of sin and spiritual death.[2] They did not hesitate but dropped their

---

[2] John Walvoord, Roy B. Zuck, *The Bible Knowledge Commentary, New Testament* (Colorado Springs: David C. Cook, 1983), 108.

nets and came to the shore to join Jesus. They continued down the shore and came upon James and John, whom Jesus also called. Now these four fishermen are walking with their Lord.

At this point in Peter's life, it would be hard to realize he would become a great man of God. This is so true of us. The Lord takes us right where we are out of the sea of humanity and creates a new person, which only He can do.

The next occurrence of Simon is found in Matthew 8:14–15 and Mark 1:29–31. The disciples traveled with Jesus to Capernaum. They went into the synagogue on the Sabbath, and Jesus preached and delivered a man from being possessed by a demon. Afterward, they went to Peter's house to have the Sabbath meal. Upon entering the house, they were met with great concern as Peter's mother-in-law was extremely ill with a fever. Mark's Gospel tells us they mentioned her to Jesus (Mark 1:30). Jesus went in and took her hand, and the fever left her. Note: She then got up and served them. Word spread rapidly, and many came for healing.

Mark 3:9 mentions Jesus directing the disciples to make sure a boat was prepared for Him, as He knew the crowd would become large and gather close to Him. He needed a place to be safely away from them yet close enough for them to hear His message. Luke records that Jesus spotted Peter's boat (Luke 5:3–11) and got in, and they steered out into the Sea of Galilee a short distance, and He resumed His teaching.

Upon completion, Jesus asked Simon to move the boat out deeper and then to cast their nets to catch some fish. Simon questioned this, as he had been fishing all night during the prime time for the fishing, and this was not a suitable time; however, he obeyed Jesus through faith and not of his own knowledge. By being obedient to the master fisherman, they filled both Peter's and James and John's boats to the point the boats began to sink with the weight of the fish. Now that is a lot of fish.

Jesus used this miracle to teach His new disciples. The one who stood out was Simon Peter, for here is where Jesus convicted him. Simon Peter fell at the feet of Jesus and cried out for the Lord to go away, as he was a sinful person (Luke 5:8). This was the first great occurrence of Peter, to see himself as he really was. Here is where he realized that this Jesus, Who was calling him to follow Him, was truly the Master over the earth. His eyes were opened to see himself as sinful, humiliated, and filled with guilt.

This is also where Simon Peter confessed to Jesus his unworthiness to ever be in His presence. Jesus responded that he should not be fearful, for he was now going to be catching men (Luke 5:10). This is a turning point in Peter's life and a fitting example for us. Jesus sees beyond our sins and our past. He accepts us where we are when we call out to Him, repent of those sins, and ask Him to come into our lives as our one and only Savior. Each of us then becomes a new person, and Jesus has a purpose for us. This is where Jesus told Peter that he would be a fisher of men. The craggy rock we met at the beginning is growing and becoming a little smoother.

We cannot forget Andrew, who brought Simon to Jesus for Him to begin a good work in him. Andrew will fade, and Simon Peter will emerge. This is also a great lesson for us, as we can also bring others to Christ wherever we may be. It can be in a senior care facility, sharing Jesus with people on the threshold of eternity, or it may be at home when the pest control person has a story to share that you can turn into a Jesus moment. It can be working with children, volunteering to serve. It can be anytime and anywhere. We just need to be prepared with the Gospel and eager to share that Good News. Do you say, "I can't do this?" I don't know that scripture.

Jesus knew Peter's limitations and weaknesses; however, He saw what this sinful fisherman could become, trained by Him. There is no excuse. I had been in church for a few years but really did not know God's Word. Then the Lord did what He does so well: He transferred us to a new place, where I joined the Junior Auxiliary and became involved in the chapter there. One of the ladies reached out to me and invited me to a Bible study. I said yes and spent the next seven years learning God's Word, verse by verse. This then led to facilitating studies in our church, which grew into writing them. You see, the Lord took control of our lives and took us to a place to grow. When the time was right, thirty years later, He moved us to put that training into His new purpose. If He can do something with us to further His Gospel, He can do it in all who hear, heed, and obey Him. I can see that. Do you see it? Have you looked?

Peter appeared on another occasion, hand-selected by Jesus. Jairus, an official of the synagogue, came up to Jesus and begged Him to come to his house, as his daughter (about twelve years old) was dying. On the way, the crowds began to press close to Him, and He felt someone touch his robe; this led to Him healing the woman. It wasn't the touching of His robe that healed her, but her faith in believing Jesus was who He said He was.

During this healing, someone came to Him with the sorrowful message that Jairus's daughter had died, and Jesus's service was no longer needed. Jesus issued a prophetic word to the messenger when He told him to not be fearful, but by believing in Him, she would be healed (Luke 8:50). Now, notice in verse 51, Jesus personally selected who would go with Him to see the girl, being Peter, James, and John. This is the first inkling of who Jesus was choosing to be those disciples closest to Him. Here we will see a dramatic miracle as the paid mourners had already arrived, along with family and friends. The child's body had been prepared for burial that same day, as was Jewish custom, except on Shabbat, the Jewish Sabbath. Walking through the crowd of believers, Jesus told them to stop crying, for she was not dead but asleep (Luke 8:52). They laughed at Him. He ignored them, took her by the hand, and told her to get up. A miracle it was, and Peter has yet another lesson from his Master.

Peter has a new teaching back on the water. Let's look to see Peter's growth. This occurred after the miracle of the feeding of the five thousand. Jesus ordered the disciples to get into the boat and go ahead of Him to the other side, while he was alone in prayer with the Father. Time elapsed, and night had fallen, along with the winds picking up, and the waves began to rock the boat. During the fourth watch (3–6 a.m.), those on the boat saw Jesus walking toward them on the water (Matthew 14:21–32). This would be a distance of three to three and a half miles (the lake is sixty-four square miles). They thought they were seeing a ghost until Jesus called out to them and told them it was He and to not be fearful.

Here is where Peter's faith would be tested; he spoke up and said, "'Lord, if it be thou, bid me come unto thee on the water.' And he said, 'Come'"[3] (Matthew 14:28–29 KJV).

Peter, in faith, got out of the boat and began walking toward Jesus. Suddenly, Peter's faith was challenged by the winds' effect on the water, and he began to sink. Why? He took his eyes off Jesus and only saw what was between them; what only the physical eyes saw, and his fear returned. Fearful, Peter cried out for the Lord to save him. Jesus stretched out His hand and grabbed hold of the faltering disciple, identifying his low level of faith and doubting Him (Matthew 14:31 KJV). Note that Jesus rebuked Peter's level of faith. Peter had two choices: a) to trust his human sense, or b) to trust Jesus. Peter started strong and finished weak; however, he did seek Jesus's intervention when he began to sink.

What lesson is taught here both to Peter and us? We go through the storms of life for Him to teach us just what He was trying to teach Peter. We are to trust Jesus alone and obey His Word, no matter what circumstances we find ourselves in. Remember: He loves us and wants us to be more like Him, which takes lessons in life to accomplish. By the way, the winds calmed once they were back on the boat, and that is what happens when we allow Him to walk us through the turmoil of life.

We see growth in Peter when Jesus asked His disciples, "Who do people say the Son of Man is?" In verse 15, the conversation shifts to Peter, who said, "You are the Christ, the Son of the living God." I love Jesus's reply: "Blessed are you, Simon Bar Jona [Simon son of John] because flesh and blood did not reveal this to you, but My Father who is in heaven. I also say to you that you are Peter, and upon this rock I will build My church; and the gates of Hades will not overpower it. I will give you the keys to the kingdom of heaven; and whatever you bind on earth shall have been bound in heaven, and whatever you loose on earth shall have been loosed in heaven"[4] (Matthew 16:13, 15, 17–19 NASB). This, my friends, is a huge turning point for Peter, but it is also very debatable. Let's break it down as best we can:

- Peter now acknowledges Jesus's deity.
- Peter (*Petros*: masculine) was strong like a rock, but here Jesus changed the meaning when He said, "on this rock" (*petra*, feminine). You see He is using Greek words, which say that Jesus is now going to build His church on Peter's confession: "You are the Christ, the Son

---

[3] J. Gilchrist Lawson, *The Christian Worker's New Testament and Psalms, Authorized King James Version* (Grand Rapids, Michigan: Zondervan Bible Publishers, 1981), 25.

[4] Charles Caldwell Ryrie, *Ryrie Study Bible, New American Standard Bible* (Chicago: Moody Press, 1995), 1543–44.

of the living God"[5] (Matthew 16:16 NASB). Looking at 1 Corinthians 3:11, Paul confirms that only Christ can lay the church's foundation.

- Jesus commended him for speaking the truth, blessed him, and affirmed to him that this declaration was revealed to him by God, the Father in heaven.
- Peter is showing that more crags have been smoothed out of the rock.
- Jesus Christ would be the builder and head of this church (Ephesians 1:22; Colossians 1:18; 1 Peter 2:6). Note that this is the first use of the word *church* (vs. 18) in the New Testament. It comes from the Greek word *ekklesia* (ek-klay-see-uh), from which the word *ecclesiastical* is derived, which means "pertaining to the church." Jesus was introducing something new.
- His church would unite both Jew and gentile to form a new body (Ephesians 2:11–3:12; Galatians 3:28).
- Christ would be the chief cornerstone, as spoken of in Isaiah 28:16.
- The believers would be "living stones" (1 Peter 2:4–5).
- There would be a "oneness" of God (Ephesians 4:1–6) that would reveal love and unity to the world (John 17:20–26).
- Peter would be given the keys, which represent opening the door of salvation to all (Jew, Samaritan, and gentile) who believe in Him. These would be the people of the church.
- Some Christian groups declare that this Bible passage points to Peter as the Rock. Therefore, they insist that Peter is the foundation of the church. Peter's affirmation; however, certifies that the church is built on Christ alone.

We next see Peter with Jesus and the other disciples on their way to Caesarea Philippi (Mark 8:27–33). Jesus asked them the question again of who people say He was, but this time, He uses the pronoun "I." Answers from the disciples varied from John the Baptist, Elijah, and maybe even another prophet. Not accepting their answers, He repeats the question, but this time, note His wording: "'But what about you?' he asked. 'Who do you say that I am?'"[6] (Mark 8:29 NIV). Peter spoke up. Was it because Jesus was directing the question to him, or was he speaking up for the other disciples? Peter answered, "You are the Christ."[7] Jesus then continued the conversation with a preview of His rejection by His people, the Crucifixion, and His resurrection. At this point, Peter took Jesus aside and rebuked Him. I find this remarkably interesting. Dr. G. Campbell Morgan said, "The man who loves Jesus, but shuns God's method, is a stumbling block to himself."[8] Peter

---

[5] Ryrie, *Ryrie Study Bible,* 1543.

[6] Kenneth Barker, Donald Burdick, John Stek, Walter Wessel, Ronald Youngblood, *The NIV Study Bible* (Grand Rapids, MI: Zondervan Publishing House, 1995) 1507.

[7] Barker, et al., *The NIV Study Bible,* 1507.

[8] Warren W. Wiersbe, *The Wiersbe Bible Commentary, New Testament* (Colorado Springs: David C. Cook), 113.

was still a bit craggy here, as he still did not understand the relationship of suffering for glory that Jesus was foreseeing.

Jesus turned and looked at the disciples and then rebuked Peter with this response: "Get thee behind me, Satan, for you are not setting your mind on God's interests, but man's"[9] (Mark 8:33 NASB). Jesus also rebuked Satan, himself, this way in Matthew 4:10.

The disciples were confused at this point, as they felt that whatever happened to the Messiah would return to them. They also could not get a grip on glory coming out of suffering, which they believed was not God's philosophy. Peter was still struggling with what they had been taught, and that was the Messiah would reign over a political kingdom. Jesus saw the connection they were not getting, and He rightly blamed it on Satan's ways. They could not see or comprehend the price they would have to pay to be His disciples, which was 1) surrender themselves to Him; 2) identify with Him, both in suffering and death; and 3) follow Him obediently. We will soon see this change come into view.

Six days later, we meet up with Peter again, as Jesus had selected him, James, and John to go up on the nearby mountain with Him, for He had something new to teach them. When they reached the top, Jesus transfigured before them (Matthew 17:2). Peter and his two companions see something no one else had the privilege to partake in. Luke (9:28–32) describes it in more detail than Matthew and Mark. He says Jesus came up to pray, and the others fell asleep from the exhaustion of the long climb. During His prayer time, He became transfigured; His face shone with a brilliant light, and His clothes turned as white and bright as the sun. He was changed from a human to a divine being in all His glory. Luke's description, by including the Lord's praying, is of utmost importance, for as He prayed, the heavens were opened. You see, prayer was the Lord's communication with the Father. There are numerous occasions in the Bible where Jesus went off by Himself to communicate with the Father. We will see this again in the Garden of Gethsemane, where once again Peter, James, and John were present and fell asleep while Jesus prayed.

This occurrence was quite unique, as transfigure means "change in form." It is here where Jesus took Peter and the others to witness this event so it could not be questioned in the future, to be documented to prove who He said He was. This is yet another training experience for Peter. Going back to what the witnesses saw: a bright light came from within Jesus and glowed through His body. What a sight to see, and one they would never forget.

As their eyes adjusted to this incredible sight, they also saw two men standing with Jesus and conversing with Him. They were none other than Moses and Elijah. Why Moses and Elijah in a form they could recognize? Both had previously been transformed. When Moses came down from Mt. Sinai, he showed a reflection of God's glory, and Elijah was transformed when He was taken into heaven in a chariot of fire. One commentary suggested what we all like to believe, and that

---

[9] Ryrie, *Ryrie Study Bible,* 1594.

is "conscious existence follows death."[10] Luke expanded the conversation between them to include Jesus's approaching death (Luke 9:31). This same explanation gave an account as to why all were in attendance: The disciples represent individuals who will be present in their physical bodies. Moses represents the saved who had died, and Elijah the saved who were caught up to heaven alive (1 Thessalonians 4:17). Warren Wiersbe suggested that Moses represented the law, while Elijah the prophets. Both point to Christ and are fulfilled in Him[11] (Luke 24:27; Hebrews 1:1).

Remember: Peter just a few days earlier had spoken up and confessed that Christ was the Son of the living God. This surely strengthened his faith and probably was one reason Jesus brought him along, in preparing him for his future ministry.

Not only did they see them, but they also heard, coming from the midst of a cloud, as mentioned at Christ's baptism, God speaking and informing them He loved and was pleased with His Son and to listen to Him. Peter even mentioned it in his second epistle (2 Peter 1:16–18). The disciples were so astounded by God's voice that they fell face down to the ground in terror. Jesus comforted them and reassured them and told them to not be afraid.

When Moses and Elijah were leaving, Peter, as only he can, spoke abruptly, without putting thought into his words; however, he was enthralled by what he saw and wanted to create a reason to exalt the experience in the future by erecting three tabernacles, one for each of them to worship. Jesus then explained the reason for Elijah being there. Malachi 3:1, 4:5–6 promised Elijah would come, and he did in the person of John the Baptist (Matthew 11:10–15; Luke 1:17). Yet they refused him and had him killed, as they would Jesus.

The Lord continued to teach Peter and the others as they traveled from town to town while Jesus ministered to the people. Peter found a new reason to question Jesus, a reason that is of utmost importance to us right now. He interrupted Jesus and asked Him how often could his brother sin against him and he forgive him (Matthew 18:21). Peter is truly listening and absorbing the Lord's teaching. Why is Peter speaking up and asking this question? Well, humility wasn't his strong point, as we see in walking through his life. He thought he was showing great faith and a spirit of compassion when He asked Jesus this question, thinking seven times was much more than what the rabbis required three times.

Jesus responded that he should forgive seventy times seven. Then He told them a parable to make His point, which He often did. Here, He is using a king to represent the kingdom of heaven. The king was settling with his slaves when one approached him with a very large debt that would be impossible to repay; however, the king forgave him. Yet the slave did not do the same for a fellow slave who only owed him a small amount. He did not see the gracious gift as out of the love and compassion his master gave to him; instead, he selfishly demanded the full debt be repaid. You see, this man was unwilling to pass down the forgiveness he had received, and instead, his prideful

---

[10] Walvoord and Zuck, *The Bible Knowledge Commentary*, 59.
[11] Wiersbe, *The Wiersbe Bible Commentary*, 50.

ego demanded repayment in full. He was immoral. When the owner found out, he was furious that the servant he had forgiven could not forgive his fellow servant; thus, he threw him in prison.

Jesus was trying to show Peter the power of forgiveness is not one of numbers but one brother forgiving brother. Us forgiving one another. Jesus told Peter that you don't measure forgiveness but practice it in love.

This was a great lesson for Peter, as it is one that Jesus put great emphasis on. Lately, the Lord has put this subject on my heart, and what I found is hopefully the lesson Peter learned. Take the Lord's Prayer, for example. He showed His disciples the importance of forgiveness in prayer. Matthew records Jesus's direction for praying and places forgiveness in the middle with "and forgive us our sins [debts] as we have also forgiven our debtors"[12] (Matthew 6:12 NASB), then reading down to verses 14–15, Jesus makes this a profound instruction by clarifying it: "For if you forgive others for their transgressions, your heavenly Father will also forgive you. But if you do not forgive others, then your Father will not forgive your transgressions"[13] (Matthew 6:14–15 NASB). He is making a point that we should stand up and take notice. Highlight it in your Bible. This is a big one. What is He telling the disciples? He is telling them and us that if you do not forgive one who has hurt you in word or deed, that the Lord will not forgive your sins, either. You must forgive the offender first. Do you see this? You do not wait for the offender to come and ask for forgiveness. You forgive anyway. Forgiveness is a powerful and painful subject, and Peter received the answer from Jesus. It isn't a matter of how many times we forgive them; it is most important to always forgive, as Jesus forgives us. He doesn't keep a record of every time He forgives us, and He expects the same of us. Clarence E. Macartney wrote, "There is no question about that. Forgiveness is the reflected light of heaven. It lights up the countenance of him that is forgiven and of him who forgives. I am sure that there was a tone in the voice of Christ, and a look in his eye which must have startled Peter."[14] Note that Jesus stated this was His commandment, that we are to love one another, as He loves us (John 15:12). You can't love someone you don't forgive. We will soon see Peter's reaction as Jesus looks intently in his eyes once again.

---

[12] Ryrie, *Ryrie Study Bible,* 1522.

[13] Ryrie, *Ryrie Study Bible,* 1522.

[14] Clarence Edward Macartney, *Peter and His Lord: Sermons on the Life of Peter* (Nashville, Tennessee: Abingdon Press, 1938), 63.

Chapter 1

Simon Peter Meets and Walks with Jesus

Questions

Review Opening Session

Day One

1. What did you gather about the reason Christ called Simon Peter?

2. What about Peter, the disciple/apostle, has called you to attend this study?

3. Jesus spoke more of Peter than the other disciples. What negatives about Peter were mentioned?

4. Who was Andrew, and what drew him to follow John the Baptist? What did he realize that would change his life?

Day Two

1. What new name did Jesus give to Simon, and why do you think He chose this name?

2. According to Mark 1:17, what did Jesus say to Peter and Andrew, and what was their response?

3. What was the first miracle the disciples witnessed Jesus perform, according to Matthew 8:14–15 and Mark 1:29–31?

Day Three

1. Reading Luke 5:3–11, Jesus gave Peter instructions. What were they, and what revelation was revealed to Peter? What does this say to you about your life, and how has knowing Jesus changed it?

2. What direction did Jesus give the disciples in these verses?

Day Four

1. Using Luke 8:50–55, the Lord performed what miracle? Who did He choose to take with Him and why?

2. How do you think this experience affected Peter?

3. Matthew 14:21–32 is yet another experience Peter has with Jesus.

   a. Jesus separated Himself from the disciples. Why? How can this apply to you?

   b. Why do you think Peter questioned as to who was walking on the water?

   c. Do you think Peter was asking or telling the Lord for Him to ask Peter to get out of the boat and come to Him?

   d. How did Peter respond, and what action got him in trouble?

   e. What lesson did Peter learn?

4. Matthew 16:15–19 is a powerful scripture, bringing the life and ministry of Peter to a new level, as Jesus continues to teach and grow him. These scriptures also have a profound meaning to us, as the church (believers). What affirmation do you receive in them? Where do they place the relationship between Jesus and Peter? What is Jesus revealing to Peter in conjunction with John 1:42? See also 1 Corinthians 3:11; Ephesians 2:2; Colossians 1:8; 1 Peter 2:4–6; Isaiah 28:16; and John 17:20–26.

Day Five

1. Peter and the disciples are traveling with Jesus (Mark 8:27–32). In verse 27, Jesus asked who the people said He was. Then in verse 29, He asked the question again, but one thing was different. What was it? To whom do you think it is directed? Who answered Him? What was his mistake? How did Jesus respond? Connect verse 33 with Matthew 4:10. Why do you think Jesus called him out with these words?

2. Matthew 17:2 (Luke 9:28–32) records the Transfiguration of Jesus. Who did Jesus choose to go with him and why? When they arrived, Jesus separated Himself from the others and went to pray to the Father. What transpired as He prayed? What were the others doing, and

what did they witness? How did Peter react, and what does this show about him regarding his growth?

3. Jesus made a profound statement about the reason Elijah was present. What was it? What does this say to you about God's Word and how we receive it?

4. The scene moves to a question from Peter to Jesus regarding forgiveness. How did Jesus respond? Jesus personified this again in the Lord's Prayer. Read the Lord's Prayer (Matthew 6:9–13) and look at what He is saying about forgiveness, and then read verses 14–15. Looking at the two together, what profound statement is Jesus making to us about forgiveness and how it affects our lives? What does this message say to you about where you are in your life right now? Do you need to personally address it? If so, do not delay.

CHAPTER 2

The Crucifixion and Resurrection

Passover

Jesus and the disciples have just finished the Passover meal, along with the ousting of Judas. The scene moves to Jesus addressing His disciples in Luke 22:31–32: "Simon, Simon, behold Satan has demanded permission to sift you like wheat; but I have prayed for you that your faith may not fail; and you when once you have turned again, strengthen your brothers."[15] In the first mention of "you," Jesus is addressing this message to all the disciples, that they would face trials in their ministries; however, in the second you, He is shifting back to just Peter when He says He had prayed for him. He is affirming to Peter that he would falter from time to time, but His faith in Christ would always be there and never fail him. He will also be restored and not only become the leader of these men, but many others, both Jew and gentile, as the Lord directs his life in fulfilling the purpose He chose for him.

This message from Christ speaks to us. He has a purpose planned out for all of us, and He will be there from beginning to end, no matter how long that period is. Our faith is the jewel that shines within us to go forward, regardless of the obstacles that cross our paths to discourage us. Through it all, we must keep our eyes and our faith on our Lord to see us to the end.

The Crucifixion

Our journey with Peter now takes us to the threshold of Jesus's Crucifixion. They had celebrated Passover together and were walking toward the Garden of Gethsemane when Jesus referred them back to the Zechariah 13:7 prophecy of His Crucifixion, resurrection, and reunion with the disciples. Peter once again opens his mouth. It had not registered in his mind what Jesus was predicting, so he told Him that although everyone else would reject Him, he would not (Matthew

---

[15] Ryrie, *Ryrie Study Bible,* 1667.

26:33). He had no idea what he was saying, but Jesus did and rebuked him, prophesying Peter's denials by saying he would deny Him three times before the rooster crows (Matthew 26:34). Peter continued, not realizing what the night would bring, by adding that he would die with Jesus and not deny him.

Peter could not believe he would forsake the Man of God when he had just seen Jesus transfigured and visiting with Moses and Elijah on the mountain. He thought he was solely devoted to Him, and nothing could separate them, life nor death. Peter also thought he was the Lord's favorite, but he still had a lot to learn. The crags were still a bit prominent. He had some tumbling to go through to be the man Jesus was preparing him to be. Does this not also speak of us? We think we are close to the Lord, until a trying time comes along so He can show us we still have edges that need to be smoothed off. Such was the coronavirus experience. Did your faith grow through it? If it did, then it served a purpose Jesus meant for you.

As Jesus and the disciples approached the garden, He stopped and separated Peter, James, and John to go a little farther with him. If you will remember, He chose them two other times: to heal Jairus's daughter, and the transfiguration. He now needed them to pray for Him, to not be tempted, and to keep watch, for He knew this was the time they would come to arrest Him. He paused and asked them to wait for Him, as He went a little farther to pray alone. He then shared with them that His soul was heavy with grief, even unto the point of death, and for them to stay and watch. Jesus now chose a secluded spot and fell on His face to pray to the Father. Note that Matthew, Luke, and Mark approach this point differently. Matthew (26:39) says He fell on his face. Mark (14:35) states He fell to the ground, and Luke says, "He knelt down"[16] (Luke 22:41 NASB). Why the differences? None of them were present; therefore, they received their interpretation from one who was present. In the case of Matthew and Mark, Peter is given credit as their source, but from what source Luke received his is unknown; it could have been Peter, as well. What is relevant is why Luke portrays Jesus kneeling to pray when both Matthew and Mark say he fell to the ground, with Matthew being more precise in stating He fell on his face. Actually, Luke's interpretation was different, as He was writing to the Romans (gentiles). They regarded prostrating yourself as a weakness. Looking back through the Old Testament, you can see exactly what Matthew and Mark were saying. When the Israelites prayed, they prayed standing with their arms stretched toward heaven; however, when a prayer was fervent or urgent, they fell on their face before God. I found this with Abraham, Moses, Aaron, Joshua, and more. Although I am not of Jewish descent, this has had an impact on my prayer life. If Jesus prostrated Himself to pray to the Father, we can do the same as we cry out to our Lord. The prayer He prayed that night caused Him to truly sweat like drops of blood. He was agonizing over what lay ahead of him very shortly, as the point of death was close:

---

[16] Ryrie, *Ryrie Study Bible*, 1667.

a. Jesus had lived as a human for thirty-three years and had human emotions. He didn't fear the cross, but He dreaded the pain and humiliation His loved ones would witness.

b. Jesus knew the reason for the cross. He knew He had to drink the cup that His Father had prepared for this time. He was to be made sin for humankind (2 Corinthians 5:21; Galatians 3:13), which required death and the shedding of blood.

c. This would be the one and only time the Father would be receiving His Son as the sacrifice for man's sins. Jesus will now never have to turn His back on us.

d. This prayer time was humanity and deity joined together.

Note that Luke added to his interpretation that an angel came and strengthened Him (Luke 22:43 NASB). I can just see the Father sending an angel to be with His Son. Jesus's humanity crossed over to His deity and surrendered to the Father and the purpose He had for Him.

Jesus then arose, walked back to check on the three disciples, and found them asleep. Can you imagine how He felt when He saw these men He had spent three years with, taking them close to Him, and sharing privately with them? The reason I expanded on Jesus's prayer was for you to see and feel the emotion He was pouring out to the Father and then to come to this point. As I was studying this, I became caught up in the agony He was dealing with and the reception He received and began to weep. We can allow ourselves to draw close to the Lord, as we study His Word. To draw this close is so special.

Now let's look at His response. Mark's words said that Jesus personally addressed "Simon" by his given name (Mark 14:37 NASB). This reminds me of how our parents probably addressed us when they demanded our attention. I would like to address this citation two ways: As I see it, Jesus was disappointed in Peter, who had just recently vowed to Him that he would never fall away from Him. Second is a quote from A. T. Robertson in *Epochs in the Life of Simon Peter* (p 127), "'Couldest thou not watch one hour?' (Mark 14:37 KJV). Plainly Peter did not have it, in spite of all that he had gone through, perhaps because of all this his flesh was weak, though his spirit was willing."[17] Dr. Robertson interpreted this "couldest" meaning they had no strength. Note that Jesus called out Peter and not the rest, as he was traditionally the spokesman for the disciples. My heart breaks here to visualize the disappointment Jesus was feeling. They had let Him down when He needed them.

Jesus returned to His prayers, praying the same prayer for the same amount of time. Once again, He returned to seek comfort or news from the disciples, and yet again, He found them sleeping, with no words or excuse. They evidently had not seriously considered what Jesus had prepared them for or did not realize what lay ahead. Again, they failed Him; therefore, He returned for the third time to continue His prayers, the same as before. Well, once again they were sleeping, and Jesus, this time, told them to arise, for it was time for His betrayal by Judas into the hands of the lost.

Jesus is now ready and prayed up to be approached by His betrayer and his companions, bearing

---

[17] Robertson, *Epochs in the Life of Simon Peter*, 127.

swords and clubs. They had come from the chief priest and elders of His people. His people, who had followed Him to hear His teachings, watched Him heal both the disable and lepers, and were fed by Him, were now turning against Him. They were in the process of denying Jesus as their Messiah and were instead going to treat Him as a criminal. When Judas gave the signal as to who He was by the "fateful kiss," Dr. Robertson points out here that signal was the customary mode of saluting a rabbi.[18] They then took Him as their prisoner. Peter appears and draws his sword, cutting off the ear of the high priest's slave (Matthew 26:51). This is yet another instance when Peter acted spontaneously and foolishly. Jesus lovingly rebuked his impetuous disciple and told him to return his sword to its sheath, "for all they that take the sword shall perish with the sword. Or do you think that I cannot appeal to My Father, and He will at once put at My disposal more than twelve legions of angels? How then will the Scriptures be fulfilled, which say that it must happen this way" (Matthew 26:52–54 NASB).[19] The purpose Christ was called to could not be taken care of by worldly weapons. Jesus then touched the slave's ear and healed it. At this time, the disciples left Jesus and dispersed, also fulfilling the prophecy He gave them after the Passover meal, being that they would fall away on this night, and the Shepherd would be stricken.

Jesus had taken His disciples, especially Peter, James, and John, down this path with Him to show them who He was and what His purpose was, yet they still did not see the whole picture. That is what He does in our lives. He shows us pieces, as we need them, to get to the other side. We will see this with the disciples after the Crucifixion, for they will look back and put the pieces together, framing their ministries. Just as we go through a challenging time, when the crisis passes, we can look back and see the pieces, but this time, they will be put together into a beautiful picture of the triumphant Christ.

As Jesus was taken in to be interrogated by the high priest, the four Gospels give the account of Peter following them all the way. John only said that another disciple was with him (John 18:15), being John himself. John records that this disciple had access into the courtyard, but Peter did not and stood outside until John coaxed them to giving Peter admittance so he could be near enough to hopefully hear what was happening to his Lord. This also shows how close John and Peter were. Now, this is where we see a weak Peter, someone who sometimes defends his Master, but other times, he fails and shows his true depth of faith, as if to say a temporary faith. Here is where his faith will be put to the test. How deep is your faith? Will it fail when tested by this world?

Satan knows perfectly how to prepare us for temptation. He took Peter away from his faithful friend and placed him in a "fiery" setting, as he warmed his cold body by a fire, awaiting news from his Master's trial. He is then approached by a young servant girl, who connected him with Jesus by identifying him as being with the Nazarene (Mark 14:67). Peter denied knowing Jesus and disputed what she was saying. Here he is using the excuse of ignorance, failing to understand her

---

[18] Robertson, *Epochs in the Life of Simon Peter*, 130.

[19] Ryrie, *Ryrie Study Bible*, 1566.

assumption. Now that the setting was becoming more than a warming fire, Peter walked away out on to the porch. The first denial has passed, and Jesus's prophecy of Mark 14:30 begins to unfold. Only moments lapsed before the same servant girl approached him again and informed those there that he was one of them. Peter continued his demise, denying Jesus again. One reason they connected him to Jesus was the fact that he was a Galilean, identifiable through his dialect, as was Jesus. So now the bystanders entered the conversation, and they spoke up, connecting Him with the Galileans. Peter cursed and swore as he disavowed Jesus again, completing the third denial. John's Gospel recorded that Peter conversed with the girl only once, and the second denial came from the bystanders, with the third from the relative of the slave he had attacked with his sword, as he reflected that he had seen him in the garden with Jesus. This account seems more fitting, as John was nearby when this occurred. The rooster crowed a second time, and the prophecy was fulfilled. Peter was now convicted of his sins against the One Who loves him, despite his weaknesses.

Using John's account, Peter's fears had been realized, as he had been seen with Jesus. He has now dug a deep hole and burst out to curse and swear. This is where Satan set out to sift Peter in sin and to take him and his relationship with Jesus to a new low. Peter wept. Have you been caught up in a situation where you disappointed your Savior and let Him down? Have you fallen back in a crowd of unbelievers and denied your commitment to Jesus? Have you felt like you failed to stand up for God's Word? This is the time to look at Luke 22:61. The rooster has just crowed, and Jesus turned and looked at Peter. This brought Jesus's prophesy to his mind of the rooster crowing three times after Peter's denying Him. Can you imagine what Jesus was thinking at this point? I honestly cannot put into words the pain and disappointment He felt. Elizabeth Browning described it in words through her sonnet:

The Meaning of the Look

I think that look of Christ might seem to say–
"Thou Peter! Art thou then a common stone
Which I at last must break my heart upon,
For all God's charge to his high angels may
Guard my foot better? Did I yesterday
Wash thy feet, my beloved, that they should run
Quick to deny me 'neath the morning sun?
And do thy kisses, like the rest, betray?
The cock crows coldly.–Go, and manifest
A late contrition, but no bootless fear!

> For when thy final need is dreariest,
> Thou shalt not be denied, as I am here;
> My voice to God and angels shall attest,
> Because I know this man, let him be clear."[20]

This is the last we hear of Peter until he crosses to the "other side" of the Crucifixion. He was not present at the cross or at Jesus's burial.

The women came to the tomb after Jesus was laid in it. They didn't seem to recall Christ's promise of resurrection on the third day, although he mentioned it numerous times as the day drew near. Not even the chosen three apostles, who had witnessed the transfiguration. Only the Pharisees' memories were quickened; they made sure the tomb was guarded. The women, Mary Magdalene, and the other Mary, were the only ones who visited the tomb at a distance, and later came back after the Sabbath had passed to anoint His body.

Where was Peter all this time? We do not know. Was he alone contemplating what had taken place? His last contact with Jesus was His piercing eyes looking at him after fulfilling the three denials prophecy. Now, wherever he was, tears must have flowed from his pain, his deceit, and the loss of his Master. Maybe he was sorting this all out and wondering what his next step would be. What would his next words be, and to whom would he speak them? He was truly a tormented man, weeping over his sin against the Son and the Father. Clarence Macartney points out that "Judas did what he wanted to do, what he planned to do and what he was paid to do; but Peter did what he had not planned to do, what he had not wished to do, what he had been warned against doing, what he had declared he could never do. The tears of Peter are the tears of a man who suddenly awakens to the fact that he has done the very thing he hated, and left undone the things he wanted to do."[21]

This, my friends, is truly an incredibly sad man who boastfully and arrogantly promised Christ he would never leave Him but was defeated by Satan and the temptations he so cleverly arranges at the perfect time. Have you ever been in a position where your heart was filled with the right Godly intentions, but you were talked out of it, became distracted, or feared failure? Sometimes, we are like Peter. We must be careful in our daily walk with the Lord to not be swayed away from Him. One way is to stay in His Word, pray often, and listen to the still small voice of the Holy Spirit. He might be telling you to phone someone, send them a card, or pray for them. Do you follow through or put it off?

---

[20] Elizabeth Browning quoted in Robertson, *Epochs in the Life of Simon Peter*, 143.
[21] Macartney, *Peter and His Lord*, 95.

The Resurrection

Reading the four Gospels, each report the resurrection discovery differently. I would like to use John's, as he seemed to be closer to this experience. John was both nearby the trial, and at the cross where Jesus entrusted His mother, Mary, to his keeping. His description begins in John 20:1. The other Gospels state that the women were Mary Magdalene, Mary the mother of James, and Salome, who was the wife of Zebedee; however, Mary Magdalene stands out in the other Gospels. She was the one who ran to tell Peter and John while the others remained at the tomb. She found them and shared with them that they had found the tomb open and empty. They were concerned as to who took Jesus and why. Mark adds that when the women saw the angel in the tomb, they were instructed to go and tell Peter. This is found only in Mark, and it is believed he received his account from Peter. Note here that Peter and John were together, meaning that John either did not know of Peter's denials or had not allowed it to interfere with their friendship.

Peter and John (the other disciple) dashed out and ran to the tomb. John arrived first and looked in to see only the burial wrappings neatly arranged. This was unusual, for if the body had been stolen, they would not have gone to the trouble to take these cloths off and lay them in their perfect place. This was the clue they needed to see that Christ was truly risen. John saw it and believed. It appears they still did not remember or comprehend what Jesus had repeatedly told them would occur. They were in the dark, so they went home. Luke says Peter went home to marvel at what had happened, attempting to put the pieces together. Mary Magdalene stayed at the tomb and witnessed the two angels and Jesus. Startled and elated, she ran back to the disciples to share her great news.

Paul states that Peter was the first disciple Jesus appeared to (1 Corinthians 15:5) in his list of six appearances of Christ as proof of His resurrection, also written by Luke (24:34). Regardless of the mixed messages written about the resurrection and Peter's inclusion, the most important to us is the fact that Jesus did not turn His back on Peter after the denials. Instead, he saw the heart of a man that could be molded into the one He had purposefully planned for him to be. He knew that Peter was the one who needed to see Him first to comfort the agony he had been suffering. He wanted Peter to be there and to see for himself that his Master had risen. Peter's pain and despair was now turning to a new hope and a new life on the other side.

Jesus meets with the disciples four weeks after the resurrection, while they were locked in a safe place. You see, He did not need a key or to be announced to come in. He just appeared, conversed with them, and proved who He was by the marks on His body, and eating with them. He even convinced doubting Thomas; however, Peter is not mentioned by name here.

It was during this time with the disciples that Jesus would commission them to be His apostles. What is the difference between a disciple and an apostle? A disciple is a student or follower of a teacher. An apostle is one being sent with authority. Jesus is now putting these apostles in His shoes to continue the work the Father had sent Him to do. They will take what they have learned from

Him, such as teaching, preaching, and performing miracles and signs, and continue His ministry. There was something else they needed to complete their new assignment, and that was the power of the Holy Spirit; Jesus breathed on them and told them to receive the Holy Spirit (John 20:22). The believers would also receive the baptism of the Holy Spirit at Pentecost to become His ministers.

At the tomb, an angel had told them that Christ would meet them later in Galilee. Peter and six of the other disciples (five of which are named, being Thomas, Nathanael, James, and John) went fishing, for it is what they knew, and they probably needed to feed themselves and their families, for we know Peter was married. As fishing was best done at night, they had labored all evening but caught nothing. The sun had risen. Much had transpired between the first fishing experience with Jesus and now this one. Peter's relationship with Jesus had been a mixed bag of emotions and personal expressions, both in word and action. It had only been a brief time since he had denied knowing Jesus and seen His deep, penetrating, yet sorrowful stare on the way to His death. Peter had let Him down. His arrogant boasting of promising to be with Him all the way became no more than a brief utterance followed by sleeping on the job and running for cover.

Now let's look at the other side; Jesus knew Peter more than Peter knew himself and refused to give up on him, for He had an everlasting purpose for him, thus the reason he was the first disciple Jesus wanted to know He had risen. Peter's training resumes as the Lord continues to smooth out the existing crags.

This is where Jesus takes the next step with Peter, becoming a significant turning point in his life and their relationship. This is where Simon truly dies, and Peter is born. The persistent mercy of Christ and His relentless grace will now take center stage as this beautifully simple planned meeting draws me to tears. I see myself, and I hope you will too, as this is yet another critical example of walking with the Lord.

As the sun broke through the early morning mist, the fishermen see a man on the beach, calling out to them; He was far enough away not to be recognized. It was Jesus, the Christ, Who shouted to them and asked if they had caught enough fish (John 21:5). He knew the answer. So He suggested they cast their nets to right side of the boat. As you read scripture, right is always preferred with Jesus and the Father. Jesus sits on the right hand of the Father in heaven.

They obeyed and were surprised to have more in their net than they could haul in. John, remembering Jesus had done this before, then recognized Him and declared it to the others. Peter was so astounded, he put his outer garment on and threw himself into the water and helped to bring in the catch, surprised there was no damage to the nets. When on the shore, Peter found Jesus had made a fire to prepare breakfast for them, and they ate together.

After breakfast, Jesus turned His attention to Peter. Remember: it was by a fire where Peter denied his Lord three times. Now Jesus is personally meeting with him in this warm light. Both instances were in a place where others could hear them. The scriptures do not say that Jesus took him aside, alone. So here Jesus calls him by his given name, Simon. Surely this was personal to

Peter, remembering when Jesus changed his name. Jesus now has a renewal available for the one who boasted, faltered, and fumbled his way to this point in time. Jesus speaks directly to Peter, as He closes Peter's past and opens a future for him. He does not remind him of his failures and flaws. He only sees the good he is capable of. Dear ones, please grab hold of this message. The Lord does not dwell on our past failures, mistakes, and sins. He only cares about right now and our future. The past is over and forgiven. Don't let it drag you down, as each day is new and an opportunity to be a new person on fire for your love for Christ. Remember: He loved you first.

Jesus now begins by searching Peter's heart. His first probe is, "'Simon, son of John, do you love me more than these?' He said to Him, 'Yes Lord, You know that I love You'"[22] (John 21:15 NASB). Here he is stating what he believes deep in his heart, that Jesus knew his love for Him. Peter uses the Greek word, *phileo*, which means to love as a friend, in responding to Jesus's *agapaō*, to love to the highest degree, unconditional love. Can you say you love the Lord to this degree?

Now that Peter has answered Jesus, Jesus presents His first commission to him and tells him to tend His lambs, babes of Christ, and He wants them fed what His disciples have learned from Him. Their new faith will be tested, and they will be tempted to wander by persecution, false teachers, and others. Sheep are prone to wander, and there are newborns of the faith who will make a way for others to follow. This is a big responsibility Jesus is asking of Peter.

Jesus asked him a second time but leaves off the reference to the others. Peter responds as he did the first time, being careful to not make the same mistake he made in the past. There is no boasting here, just a redeemed apostle who sees himself as he is and no more. Jesus responds with the second commission, and that was to shepherd His sheep (John 21:16). Note the lambs became sheep. The lambs were to be tenderly fed and cared for. Now, they are sheep and need to be disciplined in the faith, as the lambs will follow them.

A third time, Jesus questions Peter, repeating the previous question. Peter is becoming anxious with the repetition but does not allow it to reflect in his answer; however, he confirms it by reminding Jesus that He knows Peter's honest heart. Peter is maturing here, and yet another crag is smoothed out of this crusty fisherman turned apostle. Being confident in Peter's answer, Jesus now gives him a third commission, and that is to tend His sheep (John 21:17).

He is putting yet another exclamation point on His purpose for Peter, and that is to love, nurture, disciple, and teach His flock. He is the Master Shepherd, handing His staff to Peter, a newly commissioned shepherd, to take special care of them. This is seen in both Acts and Peter's two epistles.

Three denials have now been put to bed, and three commissions are being awakened. Clarence E. Macartney puts into words just what Jesus has accomplished with this chosen fisherman, turned disciple, to apostle. He "neutralizes the effects of sin, forgives its offense, blots out its stain, expiates

---

[22] Ryrie, *Ryrie Study Bible,* 1723.

its guilt, and offers a new chance. Henceforth, the apostle of weakness and denial becomes the apostle of heroic faith and boldness."[23]

Jesus now delivers a very personal prophecy to Peter. Looking back at Peter's conversation with Jesus at the Passover meal, Peter proudly denied the fact that he would not fall away when Jesus was arrested by boasting twice, first in Matthew 26:33, then again in verse 35. Jesus then prophesied, "Truly, truly, I say to you, when you were younger, you used to gird yourself and walk wherever you wished; but when you grow old, you will stretch out your hands and someone else will gird you and bring you where you do not wish to go"[24] (John 21:18 NASB). Jesus now looks Peter in the eye and tells him that he, too, will suffer the death that his master had. He would be martyred for his faith in Jesus, the Master Who never gave up on him. Now Peter will follow through with the three commissions he just received as a new man, determined to glorify the One Who made him a new creature, with the old passed away and the new birth rising for the challenges and blessings ahead.

After this startling conversation with Jesus, Peter is told to follow Him. He now looks back and sees John, the apostle Jesus loved, following them. Out of curiosity, Peter wants to know what is going to become of his dear friend. I can just imagine him asking Jesus, thinking, *Now I know my prophecy, what about John, as we are both close to you?* Was Peter inquiring because of jealousy? No, He and John were close even before following Jesus. Remember: Jesus chose them, along with James, on three occasions to teach them. Peter was concerned for his friend; however, Jesus responded in a way he probably did not expect. Jesus rebuked him. This should not be a surprise, as this had happened before for Peter. He told Peter it was not his concern if He wanted John to remain until He returned but to focus on following Him and clarified it to those who misunderstood it to say John would not die before He returned.

He continues by asking Peter why that is important to him. Note that John is the writer of this, as he recalled it from memory. Jesus was rebuking Peter for turning his attention away from where He wanted him to be. We should take note of this exchange, as it applies to us, as well. Jesus told Peter to follow Him. He had a specific plan and purpose for his life, and He also had one set aside for John to fulfill; however, that should not be of concern to Peter. He just wanted Peter to concentrate on his three new commissions and not be concerned for John. Two apostles with two destinies follow Jesus in Acts, Luke's account of Jesus's final instructions to them, His ascension, and the beginning of their ministries.

---

[23] Macartney, *Peter and His Lord,* 122.
[24] Ryrie, *Ryrie Study Bible,* 1723.

Chapter 2

The Crucifixion and Resurrection

Questions

Day One. Passover and the Garden

1. Read Zechariah 13:7's prophecy along with Matthew 26:31. Why is Jesus referring to this prophecy at this time? What does the prophecy point to?

2. Peter's crags stand out in Matthew 26:33–35. What do you see about him that shows this? Have you ever promised something to the Lord and backed down? Do you want to share?

3. As Jesus and the disciples approached the garden, what action did He take with the disciples? Relate this back to the two other occurrences He did this. Why do you think He is consistently setting these disciples apart?

4. Using Luke 22:40–46, explain why Jesus brought these three disciples with Him.

5. Staying in these verses along with Matthew 26:38, the agony that was upon Jesus's heart shows in His prayers to the Father. What reasons can you see as to why He was physically suffering? How many times did He pray and for how long each time? Fervent prayer is pouring your heart out to the Lord at a critical time. Have you ever prayed fervently? What was the outcome? Jesus went away by Himself on numerous occasions to pray and connect with the Father. What was the relationship between the two of them that would prompt Him to do so? What is your relationship like with Him? Is it a personal closeness?

6. Jesus came back and checked on the disciples three times in between His prayers. What did He find each time? What does this tell you about their commitment to Him and the message He brought them at the Passover meal? How do you think He felt each time? Does this stir your heart? Give your personal reasons. See Mark 14:37–41; who did He address the first time, and why do you think He singled him out? Why do you think He called him by this name?

Day Two

1. Read Luke 22:47–53. What transpired when Jesus returned from prayer the third time? Do you think this was one of the reasons Jesus asked them to "watch," as He knew what was about to take place?

2. Why do you think Judas chose to identify Jesus with a kiss? What was Jesus's response considering the high priest was among them? Why were His own people, whom He had taught, healed, and fed, now seeking to kill him (verses 52–53)? Thoughts?

3. Peter now takes matters into his own hands. How did Jesus respond to Peter (Matthew 26:52–54; John 18:11)? What do you see about this disciple, at this point, that would prompt this action?

4. Connect Matthew 26:31 to this event.

Day Three. The Hearing

1. Which two disciples followed Jesus to the hearing (John 18:15)? If only one is identified, how did you discover the other's identity? Where did each of them go, and why were they separated?

2. Peter denied the Lord more than three times. His chain of denials began before Jesus was led to the trial. When was it, and what did he say that fulfilled Jesus's prophecy (Matthew 26:32–35)?

3. List the three denials in the courtyard outside of Jesus's trial using the Gospels of Matthew, Mark, Luke, and John. What do they say about Peter in his relationship to Christ? What about you? Are there times in your life when you want to hide being a child of Jesus, fearful of how others might see you? Have you allowed Satan to stand between you and your faith?

4. What transpired between Jesus and Peter in Luke 22:60–62? What does this mean to you, and how do you think both felt?

Day Four. The Crucifixion

1. Since Peter left the trial and the eyes of Jesus upon Him, where do you think he was when Christ was prepared and hung upon the cross, uttering His last words Peter "needed" to hear? Why do you think this? Thoughts?

2. Who did go to the Crucifixion, representing the disciples? What does this confirm to you about Jesus's choice in the disciples He separated to join Him during His ministry?

Day Five. The Resurrection

1. According to Mark 14:28 and 16:7, what prophetic fulfillment was made, and what would it lead to?

2. The angel directed the women to see and tell whom? Who was singled out, and why?

3. What two disciples are mentioned in John 20:3? What do you see that has been set forth by Jesus and continues to stand out? Why do you think Jesus made a point to tell him?

4. Who entered the tomb first? Then the second noticed something specific that caught his attention. What was it, and what do you think he was seeing (Luke 24:12; John 20:6–7)?

5. Connect John 2:19 with 20:9. What was still the mystery they were yet to see fulfilled?

6. 1 Corinthians 15:5 states which disciple the Lord appeared to first after His resurrection. This is only given in one other place, Luke 24:34. Why do you think this meeting between the two of them is not recorded?

7. What is the difference between a disciple and an apostle? At which point did Peter and the others go from one to the other (Mark 16:15; Matthew 28:18–20; Luke 24:47; Acts 1:8)? Knowing this, why are we as believers called "disciples of Christ"?

8. John 20:22 was a turning point in the lives of the apostles. What happened to them? Explain your answer.

Day Six. After the Resurrection

1. Moving to John 21:1–25, where are Peter and some of the other apostles found following this meeting? After fishing all night, Who did they see at daybreak? What did He suggest they do? What was the result? What does this say to you about listening when the Lord is speaking to you through His Spirit? Are you sensitive to hearing it? What about obedience? Have you ever distinctly heard the Holy Spirit give you a direction? Did you ignore it? What happened?

2. Who did Jesus focus His attention on after breakfast, and how did He address him? Jesus asked Peter three questions, and he gave three answers. Jesus, in turn, gave Peter three commissions. What were they? Do you see the purpose Jesus had for Peter unfolding here? What does this say to you about what our Lord's desire is for us, His children?

CHAPTER 3

Peter Arises on the Other Side (the Ascension and Pentecost) and Opens Door #1

The Ascension and Pentecost

Now that the resurrection has taken place, Christ will remain on earth for forty days, coming in and out of the apostles' lives. We now move to the book of Acts, Luke's continuation of his Gospel message.

Beginning with chapter 1, we see the apostles taking care of unfinished business, carrying out what Jesus had been preparing them for, the anointing of the Holy Spirit at Pentecost, as promised in Matthew 3:11, Mark 1:8, Luke 3:16, and John 1:33. This is also where Peter takes the position of head of the apostles.

During those forty days, Jesus would continue His teachings. Let us briefly look over them:

1. His resurrection. Jesus carefully and deliberately made sure He was resurrected as a living person, by encouraging them to touch His body and eat with Him. There would be no denial as He performed these proofs in front of witnesses. Remember: after His tomb was seen as empty, the official Jewish statement was that the disciples had stolen the body and hid it. Witnesses were the key to proving this was false. It was of utmost importance that both believers and nonbelievers knew the truth; therefore, the witnesses told the world their Jesus lived.

2. His speaking of the Kingdom of God (Acts 1:3). The apostles still had hopes of not only a new spiritual kingdom but also a political one. They had yet to learn and preach of first a need for a spiritual change in the hearts of the lost. Jesus made it clear to them that the time for His Kingdom to come into being was not yet known. What is timely is spreading the Gospel message.

3. The Holy Spirit (Acts 1:4–8). As you will remember, the Holy Spirit's coming into Christ at His anointing by John the Baptist and God, the Father, was the beginning of Jesus's ministry. Now His ministry has come to its fulfillment, as He prophesied in John 14:16–18, 26; 15:26–27; 16:7–15. Not only the disciples but those who would receive His Holy Spirit, at Pentecost and into the future, would now be able to do things outside the norm to bring glory and honor to the Lord through their ministry. Note that John the Baptist identified with water baptism; however, the Baptism of the Holy Spirit would mean "uniting with" (1 Corinthians 10:1–2).

   a. Note also Luke used the word "witness" twenty-nine times in this book. Witnesses were important, as they relay what they had seen and heard (Acts 4:19–20). Today, a witness's testimony is most valuable in a court of law, for what they heard and saw, not what they thought, can make or break a case. We can all be witnesses, and we should be proud witnesses, excited to share what Christ has done and is doing in our lives. We can also share what we have seen Him do in the lives of others, changing them, and the Lord creating a new Spirit within them.

   b. Note that in our last session, He breathed on the apostles and filled them with the Holy Spirit, which was a filling for power until Pentecost. Acts 1:7–8 records the last words and instructions spoken by Christ to the apostles before He was taken up into the clouds and went on to sit at the right hand of the Father, where He would be our advocate to intercede for us to the Father. He would not leave His apostles behind to continue His ministry alone, but they would be equipped with His Holy Spirit, as would the believers, and that includes you and me.

4. His return (Acts 1:9–11; Zechariah 14:4). As Jesus was disappearing from their sight into the clouds, two men (angels) in white clothing appeared beside them and assured them that He would return in the same way and to the same place. Once again, no time frame is given, thus this is the hope we, as Christians, have and a reason to be faithful and spread the Good News.

At that point, they departed the Mount of Olives and joyfully returned to Jerusalem, which was a Sabbath day's walk of about a half-mile, to the Upper Room, where 120 people were gathered, and where the apostles were evidently staying. This was also the room where they had taken the Passover meal with Jesus. All the apostles were there except for Judas, who had betrayed Jesus. Let's look at each one of them; for some, this will be the last time we hear of them, and they each had a unique relationship to Jesus:

1. Peter (Simon, Cephas): first listed, as he would be the leader, and we will explore him fully.

2. John: He never used his name in his Gospel; however, the name John is mentioned in Revelation. He was humble and the younger son of Zebedee and Salome. He was the youngest and the longest living of the apostles. His occupation was as a fisherman with his brother, James. His mother was a disciple of Jesus and ministered to him. It is also believed that Zebedee died during this time, thus she was able to devote her life to the ministry. He was strong, courageous, and very tender-hearted. No wonder Jesus leaned on him. His nickname was "son of thunder," and he vigorously denounced false views of Christ. His intellect gave him the ability to go one on one with the most avid false teachers. He was also first in the affection of Jesus; thus, he became the apostle Jesus loved and the one He entrusted the care of His mother. Jesus also gave him a glimpse into the future for him to write and preserve for all to have access. This might have been the real purpose for his being isolated on Patmos, for the Lord to have that private time with him. When released, he returned to Ephesus, where he spent the remainder of his life in the ministry to a ripe age of around one hundred, dying at the close of the first century. We are so blessed by his writings and the hope they bring.

3. James: John's older brother, the other son of thunder was resolute, vigorous, active, and forceful. He was defiant and zealous, with a courageous spirit. He was the first apostle to sacrifice his life under the hostility of Herod and called the first martyr for the Gospel of Jesus Christ (Acts 12:1–4). James and John were cousins of Jesus, as Salome was Mary's sister.

4. Andrew: He was the brother and co-fished with Peter, as they worked together in their father's fishing business. He was first a disciple of John the Baptist. His desire to see light in the darkness of the Jewish prophecies brought him to hear John, who preached a message much different than the scribes and rabbis. Here he found repentance and the coming of Christ. Herbert F. Stevenson expressed it this way: "Andrew waited for the Messiah not vaguely and superstitiously, but actively and in living faith and was anxious to be found prepared to enter His service at His appearance."[25] He found Jesus and believed in Him, excitedly bringing Peter to join in His new ministry, friend, and future. Tradition says he was crucified on an X cross.

5. Philip: Dr. Herbert Lockyer labels Philip as "the apostle who was slow witted."[26] John's Gospel is the only place we find what little information we have on him, as the other Gospels only listed him with the other disciples. The day after Jesus met with Andrew and Peter, He encountered Philip, who was from Bethsaida, as were Andrew and Peter. Dr. Lockyer states that Philip was the first disciple chosen, even though Andrew and Peter had come to know Jesus the day before. His reasoning is that Andrew and Peter did not begin

---

[25] Herbert Lockyer, *All the Apostles of the Bible* (Grand Rapids, MI.: Zondervan Publishing House, 1972), 152.

[26] Lockyer, *All the Apostles,* 152.

to follow Jesus at this time and went back to their occupation; however, Philip followed Jesus at his original introduction. He followed Jesus because he found that Jesus completed the prophecies given in the Old Testament. This is not the Philip that led the Ethiopian to Christ, for that Philip was a deacon and evangelist. Philip, the disciple, was a Jew with a Greek name, meaning "lover of horses."

He found Nathanael, who also became a disciple. Philip was zealous with his new life and was anxious to tell others about Jesus. In the three lists of the Gospels, Philip and Nathanial are placed together. This is probably because Jesus sent his apostles out in twos, and they were linked together. Philip, the slow-witted, and Nathanael, the quick-witted, worked well encouraging one another. There are two incidents involving Philip I'll briefly mention:

When Jesus was surrounded by the five thousand and needed to be fed, He first approached Philip, testing him by asking him where they were going to buy the bread to feed the people. Philip replied a natural answer, by figuring how much funds they possessed and what it would take for this purpose. Not only that but the time of day would prevent them from finding it in Bethsaida, the nearest town. Philip failed this test of faith, and Andrew provided the boy with the goods for Jesus to perform the miracle.

During the Passover meal before Jesus was crucified, Philip asked Jesus to show them the Father and that would be sufficient (John 14:8). He had been traveling with Jesus, seeing Him, and hearing who He was, and yet he could not see that God was in Jesus. He was asking for what he already had. Jesus graciously answered him in verse 9. After Pentecost and receiving the Holy Spirit, he went out on the mission field.

He possibly died by various sources: crucifixion, natural causes, or execution.

6. Thomas: He has been called a man of warm heart but with a melancholy temperament, and a man of much love but little faith. He was also known by his Greek name, Didymus, meaning "twin," which is debatable. We find him mentioned in eight passages, and four of these are only in the list of the apostles. A fisherman, he was a Jew and a Galilean from a poor family. We do not know of his conversion or when Jesus called him. He was paired with Matthew. The last time Thomas spoke with Jesus was the second appearing to the apostles after the resurrection, as he was not present at the first. Here is where he needed proof of Christ's resurrection, which the others already had. Thomas was in a state of extreme grief and needed to see his master. Jesus graciously showed him the truth and gave him a gentle rebuke by telling him to believe. It was here where Thomas was the only person in the New Testament to address our Lord as God. Jesus inquired of him if seeing Him caused him to believe. He then added that those who believed without seeing were to be blessed. Here, Jesus speaks of us. We are also the ones who have not seen but believe. It is through these words spoken in His Word that we can believe. He later went to the

Parthian Empire (India), where the Buddhists were beginning to thrive. It is believed he was martyred while praying on the coast, and as he knelt and closed his eyes in prayer to his Master, his Master opened them on the other side. What a glorious way to go from this life to one with Jesus.

7. Bartholomew (Nathanael): Most of what we know about this apostle is rather short and told in John 1:45–51, Matthew 10:3, Luke 6:14, and Acts 1:13; all address him as Bartholomew. Phillip introduced him to Jesus. John is the one who called him Nathanael. Upon his introduction to Jesus, we find that he has a bit of prejudice in him. So here is another choice of Jesus, much like us, for we also have a degree of prejudice from time to time in our lives. Some may have been passed down from previous generations, and then some belong to us, alone. Philip introduced him to Jesus by saying Jesus was from Nazareth. Bartholomew responded by questioning if any good thing could come out of Nazareth. It seems the small village of Nazareth had a poor and sinful reputation, and the people were looked down upon. Yes, Jesus was a Nazarene but one without sin. He labeled Jesus before he knew anything about Him, for he surely felt the Messiah would rise out of the great spiritual city of Jerusalem or maybe Hebron. Being a doubter, he heeded Philip's request and went with him to see Jesus. When Jesus saw him coming, He paid him a compliment in his greeting, "Behold, an Israelite indeed, in whom there is no deceit!"[27] (John 1:47 NASB). What is He attesting to about this man? He is comparing him to Jacob, who was cunning and deceitful (Genesis 27:36). Thus, that was a great compliment from a fellow Israelite. Jesus also revealed His deity by His knowing where Bartholomew had been, being under a fig tree in his garden. Jesus had a special garden to go and be alone, the Garden of Gethsemane, and other great men of God had a private place to go and pray, as did Isaac and Elijah. The fig tree was an emblem of the Jewish nation, and Jesus used it as an illustration in Matthew 24:32–35. It was a favorite place for the Jewish people to meditate and pray, and this is what Jesus had seen Bartholomew doing.

What was his response to Jesus? He was astounded and addressed Jesus as a Rabbi, the Son of God, and King of Israel. He gave Jesus two of the highest messianic titles. Jesus responded with two messages, the first being His divine knowledge of him being under the fig tree, and did he believe who Jesus was. The other was a prophesy where Jesus is referring to Jacob's dream in Genesis 28:12–15 and that he would see what Jacob saw, and to Himself, the Son of man being the living link between heaven and earth. The Jewish people were aware that the Son of Man was another name for their Messiah (John 12:34). This apostle would see the angels of God ascending and descending on the Son of Man. Jesus is that ladder, and we, too, will someday see this for ourselves. After Pentecost, Bartholomew

---

[27] Charles Caldwell Ryrie, *Ryrie Study Bible, New American Standard Bible* (Chicago: Moody Press, 1995), 1681.

(Nathanael) will fade from scripture but not from working for His Master as a missionary to other nations, where he would die as a martyr, possibly by crucifixion.

8. Matthew: Although this apostle calls himself Matthew (Greek), both Luke and Mark record his given name as Levi, as that was his birth name, meaning "joined." He was of the tribe of Levi, the priest. It is believed he changed his name to Matthew after welcoming Christ into his life. He was also a Galilean, the son of Alphaeus and Mary. She was possibly related to Jesus's mother. The profession he chose was one of great disappointment to his people, as they despised the publicans for the Romans. He was an outcast from the synagogue, and the Pharisees detested what he stood for; therefore, his birth name was no connection to his choice of profession, a tax collector. He was responsible for securing the revenue for the Roman government. These people had the bad reputation of collecting more than required and pocketing the difference. No wonder he was rejected by his people and a betrayer of the faith. You would say he sold himself out, as well as his people, his inherited tribe, and his honor.

Looking back to his encounter with Jesus, as he sits at his business, the One whose name has been circulating around him appears, and only says two words, being "Follow me" (Matthew 9:9; Luke 5:27). These short and profound two words were followed by a silent but strong answer being that he would get up and follow Him. At this very moment, Matthew walked out of his hated occupation and into a life of freedom, peace, and joy. He became a new creature, just like we do when we walk out of an ordinary life into an eternal glorious life. Evidently, what he had heard circulating about Jesus was what his heart was desiring him to become: a man who could walk away from monetary gain and walk into a promise of salvation, guidance, and fellowship with the Master.

He was so enthralled with his new friend in Jesus and this new life that he gave a dinner to honor Him, and who did he invite? The other tax collectors. He was already becoming a missionary by sharing his new prized possession, his new faith. It was here where Jesus gave a new message, and that being the well do not need a physician (Luke 5:31–32); however, the sick do, adding that He came to call the sinner to repentance. He was offering them forgiveness. His Gospel message is a great gift to all.

Jesus knew the purpose He would have for Matthew, as he would record what the Lord said and did under the guidance of the Holy Spirit for humankind to have access into the future, proof of Who Jesus was and His message. His Gospel was written around AD 70 in Greek for the Jews and is the link between the Old and New Testament, "the Hebrew porch of the New Testament." In his Gospel, three-fifths are words spoken by Jesus. Little is known of him after Pentecost, and all we have are legends of his missions. One source says he was martyred in Ethiopia by the sword.

9. James, the son of Alphaeus (Clopas): The only record of him in scripture is when he is listed with the other disciples. What we do know is that he was Matthew's brother. John

19:25 speaks of his mother being Mary's sister, as mentioned above. He may also be the one nicknamed "James the less" due to his short stature. Jesus surely saw a reason to include him, as he had a purpose or a special talent for all the apostles; however, they are not made known to us for all of them. We have talents that are not seen by outsiders, as well. All we have of this disciple is his name in the Gospels and Acts 1:13. John recorded that all twelve of Jesus's apostles' names will be written on the twelve foundation stones in the wall of the new Jerusalem (Revelation 21:14). This is truly a blessed remembrance of them, since he disappeared from scripture after Pentecost. All I could find was that some believed he was a missionary to Spain and the British Isles. Legend has it that he was martyred in Persia.

10. Simon the Zealot: He was called the Canaanite. This does not have geographical interpretation but is a form of the Hebrew word *kana*, meaning "zealous"; therefore, the word *zealot* was attached to distinguish him from Peter. He received this label because it is believed he was connected to a group of Jewish people on fire for their nation. Unfortunately, there is not one word spoken by him or a single action he took recorded in the Bible. He was yet another silent apostle. Tradition says he died by being sawed asunder in Persia.

11. Thaddaeus (Judas, Lebbaeus): The apostle with three names:

   a. Thaddaeus (Hebrew) (Matthew 10:3; Mark 3:18).

   b. Judas (Luke 6:16; John 14:22; Acts 1:13). This was his surname. John makes sure he was not confused with Iscariot. This man was devoted and loved his Jesus.

   c. Lebbaeus (Matthew 10:13 KJV), meaning "heart-child" or "courageous one." He was known as a man of tenderness. He was one of the youngest of the apostles, and we know very little about him. The only notable mention of him is the question he cautiously asked Jesus, which is recorded in John 14:22, as a response to Jesus in verse 21: "'He that hath My commandments and keepeth them, he it is that loveth me; and he that loveth Me shall be loved of My Father, and I will love him and will manifest Myself to him.' Judas said to Him, ... 'How is it that thou wilt manifest thyself unto us, and not unto the world?'"[28] Here, this apostle is anxious to learn from his Master. He is much like us today; we hunger to dive into God's Word and feast upon the history, wisdom, guidance, knowledge, and understanding we can gain about the divine way our Lord chooses for us to live out our lives. Jesus went on to answer his question. Briefly, this is what Jesus said to him:

• The one who "loves Him" and keeps His Words, He and the Father will love him and place their Spirit within him.

• The rebellious ones who do not love the Lord also rebels against the Father, Who will not receive them nor the Holy Spirit. Jesus stressed that these were the words of the Father.

---

[28] Lawson, *The Christian Worker's New Testament and Psalms,* 151.

- The Holy Spirit, being sent by the Father, will teach them and bring remembrance to them of what He had taught them in His absence. Through this one question by this apostle, we know that "love" is the prerequisite of obedience, giving us a connection to Jesus and the Father that no one can break.

Other than the above, nothing is known of this quiet apostle, neither his occupation nor his family. As to his life after Pentecost, we only have legends that consist of missions to a kingdom called Osroene, where the king had a terminal illness and had heard of Jesus and what He did; therefore, he sent word, and Thaddaeus responded. Remembering how Jesus healed and, in His name, Thaddaeus healed the king and many others nearby. It is also rumored that they all became Christians thereafter. Sadly, the king's nephew rejected his newfound faith in fear and imprisoned Thaddaeus, along with his companions, and martyred them. Remember: this is just a legend gathered from *All the Apostles of the Bible* (Herbert Lockyer, Zondervan Publishing House, Grand Rapids, Michigan, 1972).

This is a snapshot of the apostles, whom most will fade away or disappear from the scriptures. To complete those present, Acts 1:14 records the ones most noted:

a) The women: Mary (Jesus's mother), the only one mentioned by name, would be a part of a profound event showcasing her son's fulfillment of His promise to those who would come to love, obey, and trust in Him. Surely, she was overwhelmed at this earth-shattering moment of the culmination of all she had experienced, from the promise given to her by Gabriel. The decision to believe and obey God, watch Him grow as a child to the Man of God, His painful death as the sacrifice for the sins of the world, seeing Him arisen, hearing of His ascension, and now this. Her mind must have been reeling with all those memories between the natural birth of Christ and now the birth of the spiritual body of Christ, the Holy Spirit. This is also where she will leave the pages of God's Word and go to her new home with her caregiver, John.

b) His brothers; however, their names are not given. They were James, Joses, Judas, and Simon (Mark 14:55); however, it does not say if all of them were present. Note that they did not believe Jesus was who He said He was until Jesus appeared to James, as noted in 1 Corinthians 15:7. We do not know if His sister(s) were there.

Luke tells us they all devoted themselves to prayer and worship in "one accord," being unified in their faith, as they awaited what Jesus called them there for. They were there to await Pentecost, which falls fifty days after Passover. Remember: Jesus met with his disciples and shared the Passover meal with them before going through the process leading to his Crucifixion and resurrection, the forty days of showing Himself to the people to prove He had risen, and then the ascension. Now they had gathered here per His instructions to wait until this one-day festival was to take place. The Jewish people call this festival *Shavuot*, or Feast of Weeks. This was a festival to celebrate the grain harvest. It also marked the rite of a new agricultural season. How fitting this would be Christ's ascension to the giving of the Holy Spirit; a new season would begin in the spreading of the Gospel of Jesus Christ through a new way, the church.

Peter now rises to speak to the 120 in attendance. We do not know exactly which day this occurred. His oration was to inform them of two purposes that needed to be addressed and taken care of. He felt this was the proper time, but was this the Peter we saw before, who spoke up or acted out of the Lord's will? Here he feels the time is right to fulfill the prophecy of David given in Psalm 41:9, 109:8. Let us look at what he is referring to:

a. Psalm 41:9 (NASB): "Even my close friend in whom I trusted, who ate my bread has lifted up his heel against me."[29] This is a picture of Judas's betrayal of Jesus.
b. Psalm 109:8 (NASB): "Let his day be few; let another take his office."[30]

Peter brings before them the need to replace Judas to complete the twelve. He asked that they appeal to God to decide who would be chosen by casting lots. What were the requirements necessary to fill this position?

1. Was with Jesus throughout his whole ministry, which began with His baptism by John.
2. Saw the resurrected Lord.

Note: The twelve were to be the eyewitnesses to the life and story of Jesus. We will see a broader requirement definition when Paul becomes an apostle.

Two men were nominated:

1. Joseph, called Barsabbas or Justus, was probably one of the seventy who followed Jesus.
2. Matthias: A disciple who followed Jesus from His baptism by John throughout His ministry.

The choice was by lot, which is a method we have heard of during our lifetime, such as drawing a straw or a stick from a cluster. Here is how it was done on this occasion.

The names were written on a tablet or stone and placed in an urn. The urn was shaken, and the first name to fall out would be the chosen one. Matthias was the winner. It is sad to note that after Pentecost, he is never mentioned again. All we have is legend that he remained faithful until his death.

---

[29] Ryrie, *Ryrie Study Bible,* 868.
[30] Ryrie, *Ryrie Study Bible,* 934.

Pentecost (Acts 2)

Ten days have passed as they awaited the promise of Jesus. The hour is early, being before 9 a.m., as the 120 people were gathered together. They may have gone to the temple and returned. Jerusalem was crowded with those who had come for Shavuot, the Festival of Weeks, or Pentecost. Pentecost also means "fifty" because this event came fifty days after the Feast of the First Fruits. If we look back at Leviticus 23, we see Jesus. Passover is his death, as the Lamb of God (John 1:29, 1 Corinthians 5:7), followed by the Feast of First Fruits, Christ's resurrection (1 Corinthians 15:20–23; Leviticus 23:10–14), and now fifty days later, Pentecost becomes the new birth, the church.

The hour has come for all these to see and hear as the Holy Spirit makes His entrance. The Holy Spirit had been a part of creation, the worship in the Old Testament, and in the life of Jesus. Now the Lord was sending some profound changes:

1.   The Holy Spirit would dwell within the people.
2.   That dwelling would be permanent, not as it was in the Old Testament upon the prophets.

The prophecy is now ready to be fulfilled, as Jesus has died, resurrected, and returned to heaven, just as He said.

A.   They heard a sound like a mighty wind coming from heaven and filled the entire place so all would hear it. I could find no description that we can relate to except maybe the noise like a tornado might make, but that is just a guess; however, it was loud enough to startle those present. Note that in Holy Spirit, the word "Spirit" is the same as "wind" in both Hebrew and Greek (*pneuma* relates to *pnoe*, meaning "breath"). They heard the arrival of the Holy Spirit. Can you imagine what they were thinking as the Spirit entered the room and announced His appearance?

B.   Then they saw "tongues as of fire." Note that the phrase "as of fire" is used. It was not actual fire but resembled fire as it fell upon each one present. Look all the way back through the Old Testament; God used fire to display Himself to Abraham when the Lord made His covenant with him, then to Moses in the burning bush, and He led the Israelites by night as a pillar of fire. He is now using the image of fire in planting the tongues. What were these tongues? They were actual known languages that were spoken by the Jews who had come from other places to attend Pentecost. When the gift of tongues fell upon one of those present, he might not have understood what he was saying, but someone else heard it and understood it, as it was his language. What a powerful experience that both outside and in the Upper Room, others could hear it, and they came together with the 120. They could not believe that Galileans were speaking their language. Acts 2:9–11 lists all the places these people had come from, so you can imagine how many languages or dialects were present. The Spirit gave them utterance. You see, when a person spoke in a language he did not know, there was another present to interpret it.

C. Those who believed in Jesus Christ as their Messiah were all filled with the Holy Spirit.

D. They were sealed by the Holy Spirit into a permanent relationship with Jesus and the Father.

Can you picture this great miracle, the promise of Jesus fulfilled on a day both Jew and gentile will never forget? Can you feel the excitement as the Spirit continued to give utterance? Some say only the apostles received the Spirit, and others all 120; however, Acts 2:4 states that they were all filled. Of course, there is always a dissident in a crowd when the power of God is displayed; there happened to be Jews who refused to believe and mocked them by suggesting they had drunk too much wine. God will not be mocked. He won this one, for it marked a universal new word: the "church" was born.

The Rock Takes the Stage

Before Jesus ascended, He asked Peter to fulfill three commissions. It is here where he takes Jesus's request and steps up to make it his purpose. Peter spoke up, alongside the apostles, and challenged the dissenters mentioned above. He pointed out that this was only the third hour of the day, which would be 9 a.m., on a feast day; abstaining from food and drink was customary before the hour of 10, at the earliest.

He now began his first sermon that, with the arrival of the Holy Spirit, would mark the formation of the church. The delivery was in the customary Aramaic language, as a Jew to the Jews on a Jewish holiday. Although some gentiles were present, the indwelling would not include them until Peter's upcoming visit with Cornelius.

We will break down Peter's sermon in three segments to see the full content:

1. The Spirit has arrived (Acts 2:14–21). Through the leading of the Holy Spirit, Peter quotes Joel 2:28–32. In reading this prophecy, only a portion was fulfilled at this time, for the rest is yet to come. Peter was led to quote this for a reason. Only Joel's verses (Joel 28—29) were realized: "'And it shall be in the last days,' God says, 'That I will pour forth of My Spirit on all mankind; and your sons and your daughters shall prophesy, and your young men shall see visions, and your old men shall dream dreams; even on My bond slaves, both men and women, I will in those days pour forth of My Spirit, and they shall prophesy,'"[31] referring to the outpouring of the Holy Spirit. He is telling them that the Holy Spirit spoken of by Joel, who had received it as a prophet, is now here. The Spirit has arrived, and 120 Jews, both men and women, now have what Moses, David, and the great prophets had

---

[31] Ryrie, *Ryrie Study Bible,* 1729.

that empowered them. Jesus came and prepared the way, leaving this earth with the same Spirit that empowered His ministry. Verse 21 (Joel 2:32) is significant for us to hold on and cling to, as it expressed that whoever calls upon the name of the Lord would be delivered.

2. What brought this great gift to God's people? Beginning in Acts 2:22, Peter now gives four reasons to recognize and accept Jesus had risen. For by this, they could believe and be saved.

    a. The person of Jesus (verses 22–24). The miracles Jesus performed were for the purpose of verifying who He was to His people. The Crucifixion was God's plan and was necessary. The Jews, assisted by the gentiles (Romans), carried it out, and this horrid death fulfilled a portion of God's plan in bringing salvation to His people.

    b. The prophecy of David (verses 25–31). Peter now quotes another prophecy, but this came from David (Psalm 16:8–11). He used this prophecy to point out that it referred to Christ and not himself. He is pointing to the resurrected Christ, who had lived and was raised to return to heaven so that the Spirit could be sent. He is also stressing that David could not be speaking of himself because David died and is buried right there on Mt. Zion.

    c. The witness of the believers (verse 33). There were five times the apostles stated they had seen (witnessed) the resurrected Christ (Acts 2:32, 3:15, 5:32, 10:39–41, 13:30–31). They saw, and they believed.

    d. The arrival of the Holy Spirit (vs. 33—35). Peter made it truly clear that the only way the Holy Spirit could have arrived is through Jesus's resurrection and ascension. Luke 24:49 recorded Jesus saying, at His ascension, to His apostles that He was sending what His Father had promised, being the Holy Spirit, and for them to stay and wait. He backed his statement by quoting Psalm 110:1, which also verifies, through David, that this could only apply to Jesus, Who now sits at the right hand of the Father, awaiting the time when He will return. Until then, there will still be a person of the divine trinity on this earth, serving the will of the Father and the Son. Now, isn't that encouraging and refreshing to be assured of each day of our lives?

3. Peter stresses Jesus for who He was and is declaring that they had crucified the Lord, the Christ, and their Messiah. I can see Peter's burning eyes as he speaks out to them, convicting them of Christ's deity, to the God they had worshipped since their father, Abraham. Now they must stand up, take notice, and accept the fact that the Messiah they had been longing for had been with them on this earth and in their presence for thirty-three years. This is from Peter, a good Jew, who knew the scriptures so well that he could call them out to them. This was the day, the day of conviction, the day of the church to be born and a time to move forward as a new people, a people in love with their Lord, Jesus Christ.

At the conclusion of this new life-turning event for Peter, we read of the response from those who heard it. I would like to think they were spellbound, in awe. And that is exactly what we see when they responded to Peter and the apostles, asking what they must now do. Can you feel the urgency as their eyes are opened and their hearts pricked with conviction?

Pausing, Peter saw that the Holy Spirit was present and working, as he convicted them and was moved to answer them in the only way Christ would. Peter answered them in three parts:

1. Repent (confess their sins) and change from rejecting Him to embracing Him.
2. Be baptized in the name of Jesus Christ for the forgiveness of their sins. Baptism here does not say they must be baptized to receive salvation; however, it is saying that it is an outward sign identifying themselves with Jesus Christ as their Messiah in their lives.
3. They will receive the gift of the Holy Spirit, the product of salvation through faith and believing in Jesus Christ.

Peter then gives them a timeless promise and that is the gift of the Holy Spirit, which is a promise from God and not just for them on site, but for all the Jews, their descendants, and for all not present, the gentiles. He continues to encourage them by sharing the Word with them and urging them to trust Jesus and to depart from the crooked generation that was under condemnation, being the nation of Israel.

His words were heard and accepted by many who believed and were baptized. Three thousand now displayed their identity with Christ and became a fellowship of believers, the church. What did they do? They devoted themselves to the apostles' teachings. I can just sense them hanging on every word, hearing all about what Jesus had taught them, as the Holy Spirit brought remembrance. They fellowshipped together, sharing in a new joy, a new beginning, and a new future of hope. Bread was broken together, meaning they ate together and took the Lord's Supper together. Even greater, they prayed together. What a blessed gathering of loving one another and serving their new Messiah. The joy and excitement were overflowing, probably like you felt when you came to know Christ as your Lord and Savior times 3,000. Is that experience still fresh on your mind? This church did not just meet on a weekly basis, but a daily one.

Now they have bound together as one body to the point of selling possessions and property. Some say it was because initially, they thought the Lord was coming very soon, and they would have no need of those things; however, it is also plausible as many were from far away who stayed behind to be a part of this great fellowship. They were still adding more new souls, which also had to be fed. A loving and caring friendship knew no strangers. Scripture tells us they met daily, cared for one another, saved souls, and read scriptures each day. Can you imagine how powerful their testimonies were? If we allow the Lord to take over our lives daily and not just one day a week, would we not be amazed at what God would be doing throughout the days of our lives? This is what our country and world need right now, for God's children to come together in His name, not just by attending worship on Sunday, but more often, like we are doing by diving into His Word and committing ourselves to the scriptures, then putting into action what we are learning.

Chapter 3

Peter Arises on the Other Side (the Ascension and Pentecost) and Opens Door #1

Questions

Day One. The Ascension (Acts 1:1–11)

1. In verse 1, Luke reveals that this writing is a continuation of his previous composition, being the Gospel of Luke. Reading verses 2–5, what period was he covering, and what were the points he was making?

2. He quoted Jesus in verses 4–5. Why did he choose this quote?

3. The apostles asked Jesus a question in verse 6. His final words (verses 7–8) to them are broken down in three parts. Describe each part as you understand it.

4. Verses 9–11 concludes the ascension. What did the apostles see and hear? What assurance does it give to you?

Day Two. Peter Takes the Reins (1:12–26)

1. Where did the apostles go after Christ had ascended back into heaven? Who were waiting for them and how many? What had they been doing (Acts 1:14)?

2. Who addressed them?

   a. Reading Psalm 41:9 and 109:8 along with Acts 1:16–22, what was Peter's first duty as head of the apostles?

   b. Do you think he was being led by the Lord? Why else would he take this action as his first upon returning from the ascension?

   c. Who was chosen, and how did he qualify?

Day Three. Pentecost: Birth of the Church (Acts 2)

1. How did the Holy Spirit make His presence known to them, and what were they doing at this time?

2. Describe verses 3–12, as you understand it. What affect did it have on them (verses 7–8)?

3. Verse 13 is what the outsiders explained it as. Why do you think they responded this way, and who were they? Do you see a resemblance today of those people?

Day Four. The Rock Takes the Stage

1. Using verses 14–16, how does Peter open his first sermon?

2. What was the prophecy he was excited to proclaim as being partially fulfilled? What part is yet to be fulfilled?

3. Reading verses 22–23, what is Peter reminding them of about Jesus, and how did God respond in verse 24?

4. Peter once again referred to two prophecies by David (Psalm 16:8–11; Psalm 110:1) for two purposes. What were they, and why was Peter making this comparison between David and Jesus?

5. Verse 36 was a profound statement from Peter to his people. What was it?

Day Five. The Response to Peter's Sermon (Verses 37–47)

1. How did the people respond, and what was Peter's answer?

2. What does his answer mean to you personally? Have you arrived at this point in your relationship with Christ and received His personal gift? How many initially came to become the church (verse 41)?

3. Verses 42–47 tells what these new believers did after their baptisms. What do you see about them that is symbolic of our churches today? Can you sense their emotions?

4. Verse 47 gives the result that we should participate in eagerly today. What were they doing?

CHAPTER 4

Peter and John: A Miracle and an Exhortation

Acts 3

A new Peter had emerged since his breakfast on the beach with his Savior. The crags are gradually being smoothed over, with much yet to go. The Holy Spirit has come into his life, or should I say Jesus in Spirit. He may be on the throne in heaven, but His Spirit is residing and working in this apostle. Jesus met him at the crossroads, giving Peter an opportunity to replace the past with a dynamic present and future. We saw him ignite this new opportunity in the Upper Room, as he became the instituter of the church.

Peter is now excited about the new purpose offered to him by Jesus. We will see it transform a life and convict a people. Now we will visit him, along with his dear friend John, around 3 p.m., going to the temple for prayers before the evening sacrifice. They came upon the Beautiful Gate, known to be the Eastern Gate, leading from the Court of the Gentiles into the temple. This gate was called beautiful because it was made of Corinthian brass and covered in plates of silver and gold. What a sight it must have been, shining in the sunlight. Its entryway was also a prime spot for the needy to beg for alms, and such was the case of a man who had been lame since birth and now was around forty years old. He had never walked and relied on friends to bring him to this spot daily to do all he knew to get funds to survive on. He would put his hand out when worshippers passed through, hoping for at least some coppers and pennies. This little man caught Peter's attention as he saw his arm thrusting out a hand for alms. Most just pass by or maybe fling a few coins at him, but this man, Peter, stopped, looked straight at him, and spoke to him, telling him to look at them. Peter looked and saw what he knew his Master would do. He felt compassion and sympathy; he wanted to help him, just like Jesus. The man immediately paid attention to them, probably expecting a pittance from them; however, Peter had much more than alms to give him, and he prefaced it by saying to him, "Silver or gold I do not have"[32] (Acts 3:6 NIV). What Peter

---

[32] Barker, et al., *The NIV Study Bible*, 1652.

was now going to give him was what the Lord had for him, something silver and gold could not purchase. He was giving him "faith" in the name of the one and only great Healer, Jesus Christ, Who would heal him there and now. Peter finished out his command to him, "but what I have I give you in the name of Jesus Christ of Nazareth, walk"[33] (Acts 3:6 NIV). The power of the name of Jesus then entered him, as Peter took the man's right hand and pulled him up. Immediately, he felt his feet and ankles strengthen, as the healing power of Jesus flowed into him. He instantly jumped up, stood upright, and began to take steps. Can you imagine what he was experiencing for the first time in his life? He was a new man, so thrilled that he went into the temple with Peter and John, praising God all the way.

What was God's purpose in this miraculous healing, the first since Christ's ascension? Remember God's purpose for His apostles? It was to be "like Him," and here they are following through. Not only was a healing taking place, others, who had seen the man begging for years, witnessed it. So they ran to them at Solomon's Colonnade, where an even larger crowd began to gather around them. This miracle was not just for the man, which was temporary, as his earthly life would end in time; it was for those around him to see a person filled with the Holy Spirit, the Spirit Who had lived in Jesus, to now see Him alive in one who is attached to Him. They could also have this miracle that provides eternal life. Peter is amplifying the work of Jesus, now in heaven with the Father.

Peter saw this as an opportunity to preach, much like at Pentecost. He knew his audience were Jews and was careful in his delivery, wisely using their denial of Christ to remind them of the crime against their Messiah. He walked them through this in such a way to show them this miraculous healing was despite what they had done. He opened by asking those who had witnessed the miracle why would they be amazed. It was not by their own power but Jesus, the Son of the God of their fathers, Abraham, Isaac, and Jacob, to whom they related. Peter made a point to call Jesus by names they could identify with, boldly indicting them for their crimes against Him.

God's servant, the "Servant of Yahweh" (Isaiah 42:1, 49:6–7, 52:13, 53:11), was exalted by the God of their ancestors, Who they delivered to Pilate. The holy and righteous One (Psalm 16:10) identified an important aspect of Who He was. They had disowned Him and had a murderer released in His place.

The Author (Prince of life, the divine originator of life: John 10:10; Psalm 36:9) was killed by them; however, He was raised back to life from the dead. Peter stressed here that they, the apostles, were witnesses.

Peter then put emphasis on his faith and boldness in the name of Jesus. Jesus's name was powerful. John quoted Jesus (John 14:13 NIV): "I will do whatever you ask in my name, so that the Son may bring glory to the Father."[34] This miracle was an example of showing and having faith in Jesus's name. When we pray, we must have faith to believe that what we ask in His name is heard

---

[33] Barker, et al., *The NIV Study Bible,* 1652.
[34] Barker, et al., *The NIV Study Bible,* 1622.

by Him and acted upon by Him. Peter is also pointing out that through faith, the healing power of Jesus entered the man's body and gave him the strength to stand and walk. He had been unable to walk since birth; however, he did not need to be taught how to walk. Faith is a mighty word, and its power comes through the name who owns it and distributes it.

Peter then changed his delivery to one of hope. He told them they had acted out of "ignorance," as they did not recognize who Jesus really was; therefore, they still had an opportunity to repent. He expressed to them that although they had crucified Him out of this ignorance, the suffering Christ endured was the fulfillment of the Old Testament prophecies.

The next step was to repent. They had heard it preached by both John the Baptist and Jesus (or heard of their lessons). They had to admit all that God had said was true in the scriptures, admit they had sinned, and recognize Jesus as their Savior. If they genuinely wanted to see and believe this truth, then they would turn and put their faith in Jesus.

Thirdly, they had to be converted. Converted to change their mind and accept Jesus as the promised Messiah. By this, they can look forward to a time of renewal, which can only come from the presence of the Lord, meaning they would be part of the millennial kingdom.

Finally, Peter quoted Moses from Deuteronomy 18:15, 18, prophesying that Jesus is like him, the Moses of the New Testament. Moses was not alone in foretelling the coming of Christ, as other prophets in the Old Testament also did and announced the days of Jesus's life and ministry among them. God's Son would offer them salvation. They would be privileged to be offered it first, as they were God's chosen instrument by which would come His blessing through His Son, Jesus. Jesus was a Jew, and His Jewish apostles would become the first Christians and the first missionaries to the gentiles. Peter, through the Holy Spirit, carefully orchestrated his message to both the individual Jew and them as a group. All of this came through Peter and John's compassion and desire to make one disabled man's life complete. In Acts chapter 4, we will see that Peter's words brought many who heard to Christ, but not everyone in the nation.

In summation, these are the steps Peter presented to them that they needed to take to bring Jesus into their lives and make Him theirs:

1. Faith in the name of Jesus.
2. Hope. They still had a choice to turn toward Jesus as their Messiah.
3. Repentance. They had to admit they were sinners, see themselves as guilty before God, and invite Jesus into their hearts.
4. Conversion. Walk away from seeking a Messiah to finding Him in Jesus.
5. Salvation. The end result of the above. The one who believes will have eternal life.

Persecution Begins (Acts 4)

Peter's speech was suddenly interrupted by the temple guard, the priests, and the Sadducees. Evidently, the temple guard alerted them to the large gathering. What they had overheard that caused their intervention was Peter teaching and proclaiming the resurrection of Jesus. This was like a neon "Don't go there" sign to them. Why? The Sadducees denied Jesus's resurrection, and this public dissertation supporting it was dangerous to them, for if Peter's message caused those present to question what their spiritual leaders believed, it could demean the authority of the Jewish Council and cause people to see them for who they were:

1. The Sadducees were in control, with the office of the high priest in their hands.
2. They believed only in the Pentateuch (Genesis–Deuteronomy, all written by Moses) as the divinely inspired scriptures, which did not teach of a resurrection.
3. They were wealthy aristocrats.
4. They were liberal and political opportunists.
5. They joined with the Pharisees in the death of Jesus.
6. They looked down on Peter and John because they were uneducated and not qualified to teach or preach in the temple.

They just could not allow this mass gathering, disputing what they professed, to continue; thus, they took hold of Peter and John and threw them in jail overnight. But they failed to grasp the positive effect of Peter's message or the impact it had on those who heard. Two thousand more men believed, adding to the three thousand from the message at Pentecost. Wow. Five thousand men compiled the first church, not to mention the women and children. Satan's instruments may have corralled these two apostles, but their message of salvation through Jesus Christ fell on hungry hearts. Peter and John were continuing to fulfill Jesus's desire for them, to be fishers of men.

The next day, Peter and John were brought before quite a distinguished jury, similar to the ones who examined Jesus at His trial. Let's glance at those named:

1. Annas: The former high priest, whose name means "merciful." He led the questioning in this trial. He was also the father-in-law to Caiaphas, the official high priest who the people still held in high regard.
2. Caiaphas: His name means "rock or depression"; little is known of him except for his participation in the trial of Jesus.
3. John and Alexander: I could find no information on them. They were just there.
4. All who were of high priest descent: They were the participants in this official meeting of the Sanhedrin. Their responsibility was to protect the faith of the Jewish nation, and they carefully examined all those who came to be teachers. These are those who questioned Jesus

and then condemned Him to death. Can you see this picture of these proud religious men sitting in a semicircle with Peter, John, and the healed man in the middle? Can you imagine the memories going through their minds and the outcome before with Jesus?

They specifically asked to know by what power and in whose name did they act upon. The stage was set, as the Holy Spirit had filled Peter. Peter now becomes a teacher, as he remembers his Master's lessons. He had already received the indwelling at Pentecost in the Upper Room with the other apostles. Why is it mentioned further here? The initial indwelling is called the Baptism with the Holy Spirit, which is a one-time act by Christ that believers receive at the point of salvation (Romans 8:9; Colossians 2:10; 2 Peter 1:3–4). This filling is always there, as we need it to guide and work within, as the Lord sees need. Here Peter is receiving that power to deliver the message the Lord wants him to present.

The filling of the Holy Spirit happens to us, as well. When the Lord places His children in a position to witness to others or carry out a purpose, He fills them fresh with all they need to go forward with a new boldness, voice, words, scripture, or whatever tool He feels necessary to fulfill His purpose at that time. Can you recall when you felt that filling and afterwards were astounded by what came out of your mouth? Well, this is where Peter is. Let us go forward into his Spirit-filled speech.

Maybe they thought they could trap Peter into taking credit for this miracle. They knew it was a miracle, for they could see the proof right in front of them. Then, they asked two things: First, by what power and in whose name you have done this? Peter, filled with the Holy Spirit, opens by replying to them that if they were on trial strictly for healing this man and how it was done, then they need to know:

1. By His name. Peter reminded them that this was also the name, Jesus Christ, the Nazarene, whom they had crucified, and God, the Father, Whom they knew, had raised Him from the dead to live forever. Only He had the power to heal the man. Jesus is the great healer, and those He chooses are the instruments to carry out this work on earth. Pointing to the resurrection was not what they wanted to hear or receive.
2. The Temple's Cornerstone. Peter stressed to them the words of David, whom they held dear, "The stone that the builders rejected has become the cornerstone"[35] (Psalm 118:22 HCSB). This was a prophecy of Jesus Christ as God's stone. Their ears were tickled by this, as they knew that the "rock" was a symbol of their God. God had made their ancestors the builder of His great temple but rejected the stone that secured its foundation; however, God restored it by His resurrection.

---

[35] Holman Bible Publishers, "The Holman Ultrathin Reference Bible," 571.

Now Peter is risking his and possibly John's life by speaking boldly, as the Holy Spirit rises within him to give him the words he was to speak to these men who had put Christ to death. He went back to the name and told them that Jesus is the only name by which they could be saved. This is a beautiful, simple presentation of salvation, both to those in attendance and the nation of Israel, for they are hearing what Peter was hoping they would receive and hold on to. They were attached to the other path, the broad way by works, heritage, and clinging to the law, which would only lead them to death. Sadly, they chose the wrong path.

Their eyes were opened to see that these two Jewish men were not schooled, nor were they priests or rabbis, but they had spoken with great courage. As they pondered their words, they began to connect them to Jesus and being with Him. Was it when they were at His trial, John inside and Peter outside, or could it have been when they had heard Jesus speak, referring to the officers who had heard Him and shared it with them? Their spirits were stirred, as they looked at both apostles and the man who had been restored, the proof of the miracle they could not deny.

A decision had to be made based on more than one truth, and the words of the Holy Spirit spoken to them through Peter were now implanted before them. The Lord used Peter to make His case and provided the evidence to prove it. The trial was ending. Fearing that the apostle's message would spread and affect the people, they decided to let them go; however, they chose their words carefully, using only "in this name," and then they went a step further, telling them they could not use the name of Jesus, either in speaking or teaching. The name they used for Jesus was "Peloni," which is Hebrew for "a certain one." He was truly the "certain One" the Father had sent to save His people. They were afraid of His name being Jesus Christ, Son of God.

Peter and John, continuing under the direction of the Holy Spirit, boldly responded to their order. "Whether it is right in the sight of God to hearken unto you more than unto God, judge ye; for we cannot but speak the things which we have seen and heard"[36] (Acts 4:19–20 KJV). They proudly refused to be intimidated in an attempt to silence them, for they knew God's Word, and those before them had done the same, as Moses's mother defied Pharaoh by hiding Moses in the basket to prevent his death, and Daniel and his friends, who refused to eat food sacrificed to idols. They trusted God to protect them. In this instance, the apostles were called out to preach the Gospel to everyone. They were being faithful to the Lord, Who called them to this purpose. God had also convicted them because they belonged to Him and not the world. These two apostles had witnessed Jesus at work, and they were to "be like Him." The officials had no grounds to hold them, plus the people were excited about what they had witnessed in the miraculous healing. Can you be that kind of Christian? Can you stand firm in your conviction to Christ? Can you speak up for Him in a difficult situation and trust Him to see you through safely? Do you listen to the Holy Spirit, do you heed what He is impressing upon you, and then do you act in faith, knowing the Lord is in this with you?

---

[36] Lawson, *The Christian Worker's New Testament and Psalms,* 167.

After their release, Peter and John returned to their own people. They shared their perilous story with them, causing a glorious response, as they turned to God and prayed, praising God and quoting David, using Psalm 2:1–2, as it fit this crisis. They were praying scripture going back to this prophetic Psalm. By breaking it down, we will see a great model for prayer ourselves, as we are seeing this new church united in prayer while facing new and dire challenges:

1. They began by praising God for being their sovereign creator of the world and controller of all things.
2. The Holy Spirit was credited to giving David the prophecy.
3. They identified the gentiles as the Romans.
4. They also identified the "peoples" as those of Israel.
5. The king was Herod.
6. The ruler was Pilate.

The kings and rulers united to be rid of Jesus Christ and crucified Him; however, God had the perfect plan. He resurrected His Son and took Him home to heaven. They had participated in this perfect plan. A powerful prayer was taken out of God's Word for this timely prophecy and giving Him the credit for fulfilling it in His perfect time.

Continuing their prayer, they moved to the present. Let's look at what they petitioned for:

1. They asked for boldness to speak God's Word, with great confidence, in sight of the threats from the Sanhedrin.
2. They asked for power to preach, heal, and perform miracles so that Jesus and the Father would be glorified, for it was through "His name" they had received the power to heal. God's supreme glory was their main desire, for through His glory being revealed, people would see, hear, and believe.

The Lord heard their praise and request, and He responded. He made His presence known by shaking the place where they were and filling them with the Holy Spirit, giving them a fresh anointing of boldness to equip them for His purpose in serving Him. Prayer and God's Word together is power in action. God receives it and blesses the one praying with a sense of His presence. Their prayers were not about what they desired for themselves but what they wanted to further the Gospel to all they could reach. This speaks to us today. Remember: the closer you draw to Jesus, He comes nearer to you, and the louder you hear his voice and see Him in action. It also gives you a boldness you've never experienced before. You see Him all around you, working His divine will.

The church was unified and voluntarily sold their goods and property so no one would go lacking. They did all together, both spiritually and materially. This, my friends, is unity, a powerful word in the life of a church, as it brings strength, purpose, ambition, perseverance, a desire to do the

Lord's will, and much more. The unity of a church has no boundaries in serving the Lord. Unity with the Lord and unity with one another in serving Him is unbreakable and unexhaustive. When we are one together in unity with the Lord, we are a family, a close family.

Luke now introduces us to a new person who would become prominent in the ministry of the church. He first mentions him as "Joseph," with a nickname of Barnabas, meaning "son of encouragement," and it is so fitting of him. He points out some noteworthy features of this man. I bring him into the picture because he was also involved in the ministry of Peter, which we will visit.

1. He was generous in giving by selling the property he owned, then brought the funds to the apostles and laid them at their feet as an offering, which was appropriate, and an apostle received the offerings; however, the apostle is not named. Looking further, Luke relates that he was a Levite. Levites were not allowed to own property in Palestine. It is believed that the property may have been in his native country of Cyprus.

2. He was among the three thousand who repented and believed at Pentecost and may have been among the seventy who followed Jesus.

3. The people of Jerusalem called him "the son of comfort," because he was filled with the Holy Spirit and expressed it in his kindness and thoughtfulness; he was an open-handed giver and freely impoverished himself for the sake of the church.

4. He was the first to offer Paul true Christian friendship after the Damascus conversion, where the Jerusalem Jews remained skeptical of him.

5. He and Paul became messengers of Christ to the regions beyond their homeland. Paul became more prominent, as they had a conflict over John Mark (Galatians 2:11–13), and he quietly fell into the background. The last mention of him was by Paul (1 Corinthians 9:6).

6. Barnabas was considered an apostle, and he had that qualification and used it until he walked out of the pages of scripture.

Chapter 4

Peter and John: A Miracle and an Exhortation

(Acts 3–4)

Questions

Day One. Peter and John's Miracle (Acts 3:1–10)

1. What was significant about the "Beautiful Gate," and why were they passing through it?

2. What caught their eyes, and how did Peter respond?

3. How did the lame man respond to Peter? What action did he take afterward?

4. How did those around him react? What does this say to you about witnessing the Lord at work (or wherever you might be)?

5. What do you think God's purpose was here?

Day Two. Peter's Message (Acts 3:11–26)

1. Peter referred to Jesus by identifying Him by three names. Give each one and what Peter said about them, using Isaiah 42:1, 49:6–7, 52:13, 53:11; Psalm 16:10, 36:9; John 10:10).

2. What does Peter put a special emphasis on in verse 16? Connect it with John 14:13–14. What do these verses have in common? How can you personally connect your life to them? What is the first step forward for a person seeking to know Christ?

3. Verses 17–18 is the second step. What is it? Peter encouraged them here, hoping to reach them in what way?

4. Verses 19–21 is the next step. What is it? What encouragement does he give in verse 19?

5. What was Peter's purpose for including the prophets (verses 21–25)?

6. How did Peter complete his message in verse 26?

Day Three. Persecution (Acts 4)

1. Who interrupted Peter's speech and why (verses 1–2)?

2. What did they do to Peter and John?

3. What affect did it have on those who had been observing? How many were they? What does this say about those who hear the message of Christ spoken, and what can we learn from it?

4. Who were those on the jury, and what questions did they ask Peter and John?

5. Who answered them, and who gave him the power and words to speak? This is a new opportunity for a new Peter. What change do you see in him now?

Day Four. Peter's Answer (Acts 4:9–12)

1. Why did Peter question them about putting them on trial?

2. What did Peter boldly accuse them of in verses 10–11?

3. What proof did Peter show them visually? Peter has now become the apostle Jesus intended him to be. Can you personally identify with him? Have you received the power he is projecting in a situation in your life? Do you want to share it?

4. According to verse 13–14, how did the accusers respond to Peter's answer? Who did they connect Peter and John with?

Day Five. The End of the Trial and Aftermath (Acts 4:15–22)

1. What did the accusers decide to do with Peter and John? What is most significant in verse 17? Why is this of utmost importance?

2. What did Peter and John reply to their punishment? Why did they release them? Are you willing to stand for Christ, as they did?

Day Six. Acts 4:23–37

1. Where did Peter and John go after their release? How were they received, and what action did they take together? Reading the prayer, what did they speak to the Lord about? Why do you think they chose this scripture to pray back to the Lord? Do you put scripture in your prayers?

2. In verses 29–30, the people petitioned the Lord for two things. What were they? Have you ever included these in your prayers? Would you like to share why and the results?

3. How did the Lord respond to their prayer? See Colossians 3:17.

4. How did all of this affect the people (church)?

5. Reading verses 36–37, who now enters the scene that will bring us to Session 5?

CHAPTER 5

Peter, Empowered by the Holy Spirit, Purges from the Inside

(Acts 5)

Chapter 4 closes with Barnabas's great gift to the church, which we just briefly discussed. He received no accolades and did not wish to be known for his generosity; however, it was important for Luke to record it. Acts 5 opens with a man, Ananias, and his wife, Sapphira, who saw the extent of his offering and were jealous of him, his generosity, and the honor bestowed to him.

They were a part of the church, being new believers; therefore, they were filled with the Holy Spirit. Their salvation was still new; they were naïve and had no reservation about what they were about to do. Satan was able to use one of his choice sins to bring the first sin into the church, and that is pride taking the forms of jealousy and deception. He knows that baby Christians are a prime target to attack the work of God.

The plan is to copy Barnabas's gift and receive the attention he evidently received from laying it at the feet of the apostle, with one alteration. They would only be giving a portion, but they didn't think anyone would notice the difference. You might call them hypocrites or deceivers, as they were planning one thing and portraying another. Their action was deliberate, as they were putting on a front to impress the church of being who they were not. They also were attempting to bring praise and glory to themselves. This is the sin of pride in action.

It is sad to know that Ananias means "God is gracious," and Sapphira means "beautiful." Their sin was neither beautiful nor gracious. It was ugly, and God did not receive it graciously. Jesus addressed giving in Matthew 6:1–4, 19–34. The glory belongs to Him and not us. What we possess came to us through Him, and when we give, we are giving it back to Him. The glory of the gift is to Him and not the giver.

Peter, obviously viewing it through the eyes of the Holy Spirit, saw it for what it was and knew the danger it would make on the church. In verse 3, he confronted Ananias and spoke truth to him, asking why Satan had tempted him to lie to the Holy Spirit by retaining some of the funds from the sale of the land. He went on to tell him the land was in their control, and they had the freedom to do what they chose; however, he and Sapphira led the church to believe they were giving it all. Peter then pointed out to Ananias that he had not just deceived the people of the church, but he had lied to God. At this point, God intervened and took Ananias's life. They immediately took his body out and buried it.

About three hours later, Sapphira appears unaware of what had happened to Ananias. Peter confronted her, as well. He questioned her by confirming to her the price they had paid for the land, knowing how much they gave of it. She agreed with him. Then Peter accused both of putting the "Spirit of the Lord" to the test (he was referring to the Holy Spirit, as it is just that, the same Spirit Who indwelt Jesus during His ministry until His ascension). By doing this, they were defying God by deliberately seeking recognition for themselves. They did not believe God would hold them accountable. Well, He did and personally, as Peter told her that those who removed and buried her husband were waiting for her.

If you go back to Joshua 7, God took this same action with Achan; God had told them to not take certain items when the city was taken, for those were for Him and to be kept in His treasury. Achan disobeyed the order and buried some of it in his tent. God revealed it to Joshua, and Achan was caught and killed, along with his whole family. Disobeying God or thinking you can say or do something without His knowledge is dangerous. He will not be put to the test.

God not only judged them, but he judged Satan, for he was the instigator, and He would not allow his deceiving practices in His church. Satan prompted this sin against God's church. God loves His church and sent His Son to shed His blood and die on the cross for it. It was created to further God's work and provide fellowship with Him. Satan hates the church and is set on destroying it. He looks for ways to do it. Let this be a warning to all of us. Be on guard. Peter was and took immediate action to purge sin from it.

Persecution Returns

Beginning with Acts 5:12, Luke now shifts to the work of the apostles that Jesus had spoken with them regarding what they would do once He had been received back into heaven. The church was gathered, not in an upper room, as they had outgrown the space, but on Solomon's Portico at the temple. This is where they had met after hearing of the lame man's healing. It is noted that no one else associated with them, possibly because of what they heard about Ananias and Sapphira; however, they did not shun them. Regardless, many more men and women were being saved and added to the church. This is the first mention of women by Luke, although there were probably many already within the church, as Sapphira is an example.

Peter's healing of the lame man and many more signs and wonders were gaining the attention of others, as they had also seen and heard of Peter's ministry and brought many who were sick for him to heal. You see, Luke points out that they were all being healed. The crowd became so large that they were lining up on the streets, hoping Peter would pass by and his shadow would fall upon them and heal them. The apostle who had been struggling and began as a craggy pebble was slowly being smoothed out by the Lord. The apostles were fulfilling the purposes set before them by Christ. Did you know that you can also be a shadow and not even know it? Following a shadow, what does it say, in its own quiet manner? Does it speak well of you, or does it embarrass you? Do others see Christ in you or otherwise? A good influence can be destroyed by a poor or weak shadow.

Looking back, we see where a woman felt that if she merely touched the hem of Jesus's garment, she would be healed. Jesus could sense her doing so, and she was instantly healed. It was not the action she took that produced her healing, but it was her faith that healed her. Whether it be by Peter, Paul, or anyone else, Jesus honors and cherishes that faith. Doctors today will admit that those who survive an illness or accident beyond what they could provide came through it miraculously, by their faith.

Once again, the high priest and a sect of the Sadducees make their appearance. Pausing, I wonder what is going through Peter's mind. Would it be a flashback of his denial of Jesus when he was in front of these same people, or of the previous episode, when he was in front of them after healing the lame man, or could it be when Jesus pointed out His purpose for them (Mark 16:15–18), to be and do what and where they are now. He learned and grew from both and remained faithful, not fading under their pressure and threats. Look at your life. Do you choose to follow the path He lays out for you? Just as Peter walked a rocky road and smoothed out a wavy life in his conviction to follow Christ, we also can pursue and live a life serving the Lord.

There was a difference in this confrontation, being that there was no questioning before the priest and Sadducees, as their jealousy had reached the boiling point. They grabbed all the apostles and threw them in jail. This is what they had warned Peter and John would happen:

1. They had not obeyed the orders previously given to them to stop preaching in the "name of Jesus Christ" and defying their laws.
2. They were refuting what they, the Sadducees, believed and that was no resurrection, by showing the people the truth, that Jesus was truly alive.
3. Their envy and jealousy were devouring them, as they watched such unworthy men divert the people's attention away from them and their way of carrying out their leadership in the faith handed down to them. They felt they were defending the faith of their fathers and not that of the one true God and His beloved Son, their Messiah, Who they rejected. Envy and jealousy are prime instruments of Satan, the great deceiver, who uses them to blind us to the truth, and the accusers were his vessels to pour it out.

Satan never rests and is always on the prowl, looking for ways to weaken or destroy our walk with the Lord. What can we do to keep the door shut? Walk closely with the Lord. Listen to the Holy Spirit when He is speaking to you, heed what He is saying, and act upon it. Believe me, He has a purpose that is in your best interest. Go deep into God's Word, as the deeper you dive, the greater and more secure you grow, and pray often for Him to guard your mind, give you wisdom, open your eyes, and protect you from walking into Satan's temptations. We must always walk in and through the Spirit.

So this time, they thought they had not only Peter and John, but all the apostles in their grasp, and their work would be shut up in the confines of their secure jail. God had another plan that showed how small the faith was of those who put them there. He sent an angel, a messenger, to take them out of the jail, without notice. This angel also had a message from God for them and that was to go back to the temple and continue preaching the Gospel. God was in control, and the accusers were denied, through an angel in which they also did not believe. Their traditions were cold and dead, but the apostles, along with the new believers, were on fire with this life in Jesus Christ. They returned at the break of day and took up right where they left off.

Meanwhile, the high priest, along with his assembled council, sent for the apostles. The officers found nothing out of order, except for no apostles. Someone just happened to enter and said they had seen them at the temple, instructing the people as if nothing had happened. So they went after them again and brought them back to the council.

Once again, the high priest reminded them of their previous orders; however, this time, he was careful not to mention Jesus but replaced it with "this man" and "this man's blood." Was it because he was strongly opposed to Jesus so much that he could not even say His name, or was he spiritually destroyed by what has occurred since he orchestrated His death and now had to face the realization that His followers and miracles were far greater than anything he had ever achieved, or even would as his prominent position would proclaim?

Peter, emboldened and empowered by the Holy Spirit to increase faith and witness, is once again the voice of the apostles and his Master. He smoothly proclaimed that God alone raised up, exalted, and placed Jesus at His right hand once He had returned to His rightful place after they had put Him through that horrid and bloody death on a cross, as he reminded them of his previous message. He is now the Prince, the Savior Who can grant repentance to Israel and forgive their sins. Peter continued to remind them that the apostles were witnesses, as well as the Holy Spirit God had bestowed upon those who obey Him. This is the restored Peter, taking the reins to fulfill what Jesus had asked of him. What a transformation, what a boldness, what a love for this Man, this name.

This message did not fall on deaf ears but ones that wanted revenge, not an avenue to a new life, a new Gospel, eternal life. They could claim their Messiah now, but sadly, once again, they were blinded to the truth.

A Pharisee by the name of Gamaliel stood and intervened. His name means "the Lord is my reward." He was one of the greatest teachers of his time and was known to have taught Paul (Saul). As a leader of the Pharisees, he held a senior position in the council and was considered a moderate/liberal among them. Breaking down his speech regarding the apostle's belief, this is how he intervened:

1. He compared them to two others who had raised up a faction against them. He pretty much said that those like them come and go.
2. These types have been here before, and when their leader died, they disbanded and faded away to be no more of a threat.
3. If they are truly of God, they cannot be overthrown. You cannot fight against God and succeed.

His suggestion was to wait and see. That's right, wait and see what God will do, for He was doing it right then by making an opening for the apostles to be released; however, it was accompanied by some beating and orders attached to warn them to stop speaking in the "name of Jesus." Note, this time they used His name. Once again, God used someone from the other side to intervene for His work.

The result was rejoicing that they had been considered worthy to suffer shame for His name. Can you feel their elation, even though they probably had raw, bloody stripes to prove it? Peter and the eleven apostles stood their ground for their Master and the purpose He had set before them. They did not miss an opportunity and resumed teaching and preaching Jesus as the Christ, His name that would continue to save until He returns.

We are spiritual heirs to these courageous followers. We are proof that our Lord is faithful and lives forever. We are the proof that what Gamaliel said was true, for if it is of God, you will not be able to stop them. In closing this chapter, two periods of testing have now occurred, as Jesus predicted, and His peace has seen them through to the other side, and that is where we are now headed. Peter has been instrumental in applying key #1 in the formation of the church at Pentecost.

Chapter 5

Peter, Empowered by the Holy Spirit, Purges from the Inside

Questions

Day One. Peter Purges from Within (Acts 5:1–111)

1. What was Ananias's sin?

2. Peter confronted him and charged him with what? What does this say to you about what you say and do having an effect with your relationship to the Lord? Do you take this seriously or think the Lord will overlook it?

3. Verse 5 says that Ananias fell dead as Peter rebuked him. This discipline came from whom, and why do you think it was so severe?

4. The scene now switches to Sapphira, Ananias's wife. What did she do that also upset Peter? What did he accuse her of?

5. Peter used this phrase in his accusation: "you agreed together to put the Spirit of the Lord to the test" (verse 9)[37] (see Matthew 4:7; Deuteronomy 6:16). How would you interpret this? This was a sin unto death. Why? What happened to her?

Day Two. Persecution Returns

1. Verse 12 switches to the apostles carrying out their directive from the Lord. They met at the temple area where Peter had healed the lame man. According to verses 14–16, what was the response they were receiving?

2. Verse 15 centers on Peter. A positive and a negative are mentioned. What were they? Did the positive attract the negative? Why (see verse 17)?

3. Verse 16 says that all were being healed. Why do you think they were "all" being healed and for all to see at the temple and around it?

---

[37] Ryrie, *Ryrie Study Bible*, 1735.

Day Three. Persecution Presents Itself

1. How were the apostles treated by the priest and his cohorts? For what reason, according to 4:18? List other reasons.

2. How did the Lord respond to this (verses 19–20)?

3. What is "the whole message of this life," and where were they to go to speak it? What do you think the Lord is doing here?

4. How did those who came for them at the jail react, and what did they do in response?

Day Four. A New Trial (Acts 5:28–32)

1. The high priest questioned them as to why they did not obey the order given to them at the last trial. Why do you think he left out Jesus in his accusation? He further accused them of the intent "to bring the man's blood upon us"[38] (verse 28). What do you think he is referring to?

2. What was Peter's bold response? Who did he mention that was not mentioned at the previous trial? Why do you think Peter added Him here?

Day Five. Acts 5:33–42

1. How was Peter's defense received, and who spoke out? What do you know about him in what you have learned in studying God's Word?

2. What order did he give before he delivered his advice?

3. He gave examples of past instances like this one. What were they (verses 36–37), and how did they relate to this case?

4. Verses 38–39 states two paths these apostles could be taking. What were they, and which one held true?

5. What decision was made, and how did they direct it to the apostles? How did the apostles respond? Was the Lord glorified in the end?

---

[38] Ryrie, *Ryrie Study Bible,* 1736.

CHAPTER 6

Peter Opens Door #2

(Acts 8–9)

Jesus had said to Peter, "I will give you the keys of the kingdom of heaven; and whatever you bind on earth shall have been bound in heaven, and whatever you loose on earth shall have been loosed in heaven"[39] (Matthew 16:19 NASB). A key is a badge of authority, and Jesus is now passing them to Peter. He is to use them to open the doors of faith and eternal life to the others by preaching the Kingdom of God through his message of the Gospel of Jesus Christ. The first key opened the door to the Jews at Pentecost, when the Holy Spirit came down and completed the salvation of those present. Now we are going to see him insert the second key and that is to the Samaritans.

Moving to the second part of this verse, Jesus is making a statement of dos and don'ts. The phrase "binding and loosing" was commonly used by rabbis in referring to if something was admissible according to the law they professed to live by. Jesus is using it because Peter and the apostles understood it. What He is saying is that they should do on earth whatever God has already willed in heaven, not in reverse, as we are to obey His will here on earth. They were to make their judgements based on what Jesus had taught them and the Holy Spirit revealed to them; therefore, they would be agreeing with Jesus and the Father in heaven. In short, Thy will be done and not my will.

We are now introduced to the other Philip, the deacon-evangelist. After the apostles were freed, the church continued to grow. It became too large for them to care for alone. They decided to select seven men, who were believers, reputable and spiritually wise. Philip was one of those chosen and a devout spreader of the Gospel. He was the first to be given the title of evangelist and the first to venture into Samaria to share the Word.

The Samaritans were a mixed race. After the tribes of Judah and Benjamin split from the twelve, idolatry began to take over the northern tribes, and they became weaker. It is easy to see

---

[39] Ryrie, *Ryrie Study Bible*, 1544.

why, for they had put their one true God in the background. The Assyrians invaded them in 721 BC and took the people captive and dispersed them. Then they brought captives from other pagan lands in to mingle with those left behind. Well, the Jews intermarried with them and adopted their idols. Those who did not go wholly into idolatry formed their own religion and only recognized the first five books (Pentateuch) of the Bible as theirs. They considered Moses as their only prophet and intercessor to God. Mt. Gerizim was their holy place to worship God. The pure Jews began to separate from them under the leadership of Ezra. Up until this time, they were still despised and considered half-breeds. Much animosity had developed between them and the Jews, who would refuse to even go through their land when traveling. Jesus was the first to resolve this on several instances.

1. Jesus was passing through on His way to Jerusalem just before His ascension and wanted to stop by a Samaritan village; however, they refused Him. James and John asked Him if they could order fire to come and extinguish them? Jesus rebuked them for it.
2. Jesus honored a Samaritan for his hospitality.
3. Jesus praised a Samaritan leper for his gratitude.
4. Jesus healed Samaritan lepers.
5. Jesus witnessed to a Samaritan woman at the well.
6. Jesus asked the disciples to witness to them.

Now that we recognize who they were, Philip crossed over to the city of Samaria, which was about forty miles north of Jerusalem, and began sharing Christ with them. This is the first outreach of the church. He had the gifts of signs, removing unclean spirits (demons), and healing. They believed and were baptized in the name of Jesus and delivered from their sins; however, they did not receive the Baptism of the Holy Spirit at this time. Why? The Samaritans were unaware of the promise of the Holy Spirit taught by Jesus and did not know what had transpired at Pentecost; therefore, Peter and John, being apostles, only had the authority to testify it to them and bestow this gift of Jesus. The Samaritans now would receive the fullness of the Holy Spirit, by both praying and laying on of hands by them. This was necessary to bring these new people into God's church and a warning to prevent them from establishing their own church. Door #2 was now opened by Peter, with John by his side.

There was a man in Samaria named Simon. He was a magician who was attracting the people until they were distracted by Philip's preaching, performing signs, delivering people from unclean spirits, and healing. So Simon decided to follow them and was baptized; however, he saw what Peter and John were doing and wanted the Holy Spirit, as well. Something was very wrong with his motive. He wanted it selfishly, for his own gain. It is evident Simon was not saved at all, just a copycat with selfish intentions, and Peter saw it.

Two Simons, face to face. One dedicated to the service of his Master, and the other, a clever deceiver, wrapped up in false doctrine and sin. Sounds somewhat like Ananias and Sapphira, with a little Judas Iscariot mixed in. Let's look at Peter's response to Simon:

1. Peter was livid as he scolded him and declared that his money would also die with him, as he thought he could buy the gift of God! Here is evidence this Simon wasn't saved at all, for the gift of God is free to those who earnestly seek Him.
2. His heart was not right with God. Simon's faith was faked.
3. Repent of your wickedness; Peter is calling on him to repent and to seek a right relationship with the Lord, a step to becoming a believer.
4. Peter told him to pray to the Lord for forgiveness, as he was in bondage of iniquity and bitterness. He was taking him through the steps to salvation and a new life released from the bondage of Satan. The Lord was there waiting to forgive him and to put this life behind him.

Instead of praying the prayer for salvation himself, he only asked that they pray for him that none of the things Peter pointed out would happen to him. He failed to receive the invitation to turn to the light of God, and we do not know if he ever walked away from a devious dark life. We can follow Peter's example and present the plan of salvation to the lost, praying that their heart will receive it, but they must receive it for themselves.

Another point is evident here: God used Peter to intervene in this man's attempts to be included among those who earnestly became believers. If he had not, this imitator would have been received into the church with the others. Peter, once again being prompted by the Holy Spirit, exposed him for who he was, and he was not received into God's church.

Peter and John began their journey back to Jerusalem. As they passed through Samaria, they stopped and shared their Good News, spreading the Gospel to the outside and continuing to open the door to them. What a joy they must have felt. Their walking back probably felt like they were walking on a cloud, a holy cloud. Do you feel that joy when you share your faith with others? You will never forget the times you have shared the Lord and that message produced fruit, fresh new souls for Christ.

God Prepares Peter to Invite the Gentiles (Acts 9:32–43)

This chapter opens with the conversion of Saul, the Pharisee who detested those who followed the teachings of Jesus. His hatred stood out as he attended the stoning of Stephen; however, after he left the scene and was en route to Damascus, Jesus entered his life, and his anger died. God used this event, along with the intervention of Gamaliel, to bring a period of peace. It also scattered the apostles, opening doors for the spread of the Gospel, as Philip, along with Peter and John, had done in Samaria.

I opened with this because we will now see Peter traveling and being faithful in continuing the commission Christ asked of him. Verse 31 speaks of the church in Judea, Galilee, and Samaria. Luke then points out that Peter is moving through these regions, spreading the Gospel and looking for opportunities to bring others to Christ. This craggy rock of a fisherman has evolved into a much smoother stone as he evangelizes and strengthens Christ's church.

He now makes a stop in Lydda (Lod), a town south of Joppa. Here we are going to see him as we did at the Beautiful Gate. Once again, there's a man at the gate; however, this man had only been in this condition for eight years. Peter stopped when he saw him. Does this sound familiar? Previously, Peter told the man to walk; however, here he calls the man by name, tells him Jesus had healed him, and says to rise and make his bed. The man immediately obeyed. People saw and heard this great miracle, and they turned to the Lord, thus adding more souls to Christ.

Meanwhile, the healing had reached Joppa, a city of many gentiles. There was a woman named Tabitha, which in Greek translates as "Dorcas," meaning gazelle. This woman was greatly adored, respected, and appreciated. She was the first woman within the church to be commended for her work. Today, you will see women's organizations with the name Dorcas. She was a seamstress and made garments to give to the poor. We have a group modeled after her in our church named Hearts and Hands, who also sew and make items for others. Acts 9:36 and 38 caught my attention, as both spoke of her and those reaching out to Peter being named as disciples. Beginning with the book of Acts, this term is used to refer to those who believe in Christ. We Christians today are called disciples of Christ. They had come to seek out Peter and did not mention to him that she had died when speaking to him, although it was in verse 37. Peter was the leader of the church and was committed to the people. They had faith in the power of Jesus. Peter had been given the power to heal, and he used that power to glorify his Lord, not himself, as his humility showed. This would be his first experience alone in death to life, as he had been with Jesus when He brought Jairus's daughter back to life. Peter did not stumble, pause, or make excuses but went with them, where he found a group of widows weeping. They even showed Peter garments Tabitha had made.

Peter asked them to leave the room and then went down on his knees and prayed. I would love to have heard his prayer. He then arose, and through his faith, he spoke her name and told her to rise up. She opened her eyes, saw Peter, and sat up. He then gave her his hand and raised her up, calling those who had left the room to return. Note that he did not touch her until God had answered his prayer and restored her, for he knew not to become ceremonially defiled (Leviticus 21:1; Numbers 5:2; 9:6, 10; 19:11). He was still adhering to the Jewish customs.

Now let us step back in time (Mark 5:34–43), when Jesus took Peter, John, and James with Him to Jairus's home, where his daughter lay dead and prepared for burial. Peter saw Jesus (Mark 5:40) revive the little girl. Jesus had prepared this very moment for Peter. The difference was, Jesus took the girl's hand before He spoke to her, as He had no fear of defilement. In both cases, this little girl and Tabitha came back to life through the divine power of Jesus Christ.

Here is a teaching moment:

1. Jesus purposely took Peter with him to witness Him bring the girl back to life.
2. When Peter was called to come to Joppa to bring Tabitha (Dorcas) back to life, he now had the Holy Spirit within him to connect him with Jesus, Who would be the source of her revival, as the Holy Spirit was the intercessor between Him and Peter.
3. The Lord prepares us for situations in the future, training us for what lies in the path ahead of us. He knows when we will need Him to carry us through something. We will have His peace, through the same Holy Spirit that connects Peter with Him.

Peter stayed for a while in Joppa, as he had opportunities to bring more souls to Christ who had heard of this great miracle. He had to secure a place to live, and he chose to stay with another man named Simon, a Jewish Christian and a tanner by trade, which means he worked with dead animals. The Jews frowned upon this trade, as they considered it and the person unclean. Tanners were despised by Jewish society. Peter was continuing to break free from the bondage of Judaism, but slowly. He is taking one step at a time as he grows into the ultimate purpose Christ has for him, and that was to "be like Him." Just as Peter was filled with the Spirit, who directed his path, we are also filled as we travel through life, giving us the most meaningful family on earth: the church, the body of our Lord Jesus Christ.

Chapter 6

Peter Opens Door #2

Questions

Day One. Philip Is Introduced (Acts 8:4–13)

1. Who is Philip (Acts 6:1–5), and what was his position?

2. Where did he go to share the Gospel? What else did he do to attract people to his message?

3. Who is Simon, and what influence did Philip have upon him?

Day Two. Peter Enters (Acts 8:14–25)

1. For what purpose was Peter sent to Samaria, and who came with him? See Matthew 16:19 and Isaiah 22:22.

2. Which baptism did they receive by Philip's message, and which one could he not impart to them? Why?

3. Simon re-enters the story. What about Peter and John impacted him? Based on his conversation with Peter, do you think he was truly saved or an imposter (verses 20–24)? This is a lesson in sharing the Gospel with others. What are you not assured of after you share it with others?

Day Three. God Prepares Peter to Preach to the Gentiles (Acts 9:32–43)

1. Reading verses 32-35, what miracle did Peter perform, and how was it similar and different to his first one?

2. Why was Peter called to Joppa? Connect it to Mark 5:34–43. What is similar between these two miracles? Do you think Peter looked back on this previous experience, and why?

3. Verse 36 states that Tabitha (Dorcas) was a disciple. What does that tell you about her? What else is significant about her (verses 36–39)? Do you see something familiar in churches today that women have in common with her?

4. What effect did this miracle have on the people?

5. Peter then stayed in Joppa for a while longer. Where did he stay, and what was significant about it? Has the Lord taken you to other places to prepare you for His purpose?

CHAPTER 7

Peter Opens Door #3

The First Gentiles become Disciples of Christ

(Acts 10)

This chapter is one that stands out in the New Testament and occurred around ten years after Pentecost. It contains two dreams (visions) by two people who will bring Christianity, the church, to the gentiles (Romans). We just saw Philip, Peter, and John take it to the Samaritans, and now the Lord is once again giving the key to Peter to open the final door, as he has already opened it to both the Jews and the Samaritans.

The first dream was given to Cornelius, a Roman centurion (a centurion was a highly respected officer given leadership over a hundred soldiers). Cornelius was in Caesarea, the Roman capital of Judea, which was around thirty miles from Joppa, where Peter is staying at the tanner's house. Although he was a Roman gentile, their pagan religion had grown cold within him, and he turned to Judaism to fill the void in his spirit. He obeyed the law, fasted, and dealt kindly with the local Jewish people. You could say he was close to being one of them, yet there were still areas that remained forbidden to him, and one was offering sacrifices; therefore, he substituted with his prayers as his personal way of sacrificing, praying often and at the times the Jewish people also prayed. He was being religious but still lost and yet knew deep within the way was out there.

The time was 3 p.m., which was a Jewish time of prayer, as this had also been the time Peter and John were going through the Beautiful Gate and saw the disabled man. As he prayed, an angel appeared to him and called his name. Cornelius questioned him by calling him Lord and asking what he wanted. The angel responded with the message the Lord had sent him to deliver. He told Cornelius that God had received his prayers and offerings as his alternative to a sacrifice. Little did Cornelius know that he and his family were about to receive a gift in return, the greatest gift of all: salvation. The angel gave specific instructions to send some of his men to Joppa to find Simon Peter (verse 6), and he even told him where he was staying. God is known to be specific in all His words, and specific He was here. After the angel departed, Cornelius wasted no time and called for two of his servants and a trusted soldier, giving them the angel's directions. They were to travel the thirty miles on horseback, which would take about two days.

Meanwhile, as they were traveling to find Peter, it was noon (sixth hour), and Peter went to the house top to pray, being a devout man of prayer. He had evidently gone some time without eating and was waiting to eat until he finished his prayers; he fell into a trance and saw the sky open, and out of it a sheet was lowered down to him. Within it was an assortment of four-footed animals, crawling creatures, and birds. As he viewed the images, a voice spoke and instructed him to kill and eat, not only to satisfy his hunger but for a much greater purpose.

A bit of the old Peter, with some crags still clinging to this rock, now comes out. Orthodox Judaism is still buried within him, and here is a place where he must make a choice, a choice to cling to the old or embrace the new. He replied to the Lord that he could not eat these things that were unholy or unclean (Acts 10:14). The Lord is also revealing to him that although the Jews considered the gentiles as unclean, He did not see them that way. Peter must have also failed to remember Jesus's words. Let's look back at what Jesus said when some Pharisees came to spy on Him and the disciples in Galilee. What they saw was a breaking of their closely held tradition, and that was eating without first washing their hands, and they took pleasure in bringing it to their attention.

Jesus called out to all present, including the disciples, "Are even you still lacking in understanding? ... Don't you realize that whatever goes into the mouth passes into the stomach and is eliminated? But what comes out of the mouth comes from the heart, and this defiles a man. For from the heart comes evil thoughts, murders, adulteries, sexual immoralities, thefts"[40] (Matthew 15:16–19 HCSB). The Lord is reminding Peter at a very opportune time that He had spoken this message, being that what He had cleansed was to no longer be thought of as unholy. Well, this happened a total of three times to remind him that he is now free from the burden of the Mosaic system. You see, Peter is unknowingly resisting God showing him that He is leading him into a new and critical opportunity that would change the world, as he knew it, and as we are blessed to be within. He has now moved to the other side, and a new purpose is awaiting him, where Peter would now open the last door to the gentiles. No longer would there be a distinction between them.

Peter was perplexed about this vision and was attempting to sort it out in his mind when the men Cornelius sent arrived, following the directions given to them. As they were approaching the gate seeking Peter, the Holy Spirit spoke to Peter and told him of the three men who had come for him, and to go down to the door and greet them for He had personally sent them. He also told him that He wanted him to go with the men. Peter obeyed and greeted them, asking what they wanted of him. They were careful to paint a picture of Cornelius in such a way to put Peter at ease and not fear him, for he was a Roman centurion. They related that he was a just man, he feared God, and the Jews spoke highly of him. He was a Roman brought up in a culture of pagan gods, yet they

---

[40] Holman Bible Publishers, "The Holman Ultrathin Reference Bible," 919–20.

assured Peter that he feared Peter's God. Then they made their point for coming, being that an angel had sent them to find Peter and bring him back to bring a message to them.

Peter did not hesitate; he invited them to stay the night and said he'd go with them the next day. Jewish people normally did not allow gentiles to reside or eat with them in their homes; therefore, Peter is beginning to see the meaning of his vision. During this time, Peter asked six Jewish men to accompany him on this trip. Why would he do this? They were to be his witnesses.

After the two-day journey, Peter and his companions arrived at the home of Cornelius, where his host had gathered relatives and close friends in anticipation of his message. Upon Peter's entry, Cornelius fell down and worshipped him, believing that the person the angel told him to send for must be remarkably close to God. Peter reached down and pulled him up, assuring him that he was not special, but a man like him, knowing that worship belonged only to his Lord.

As Cornelius ushered him in, he was greeted by a room full of the host's family and friends. Here he was facing what it was to a Jew, an unclean act to come into a gentile's unclean home. His vision of the unclean animals surely came back to his memory, and he connected it to these people by sharing with them that God had shown him he could not designate a man as being unholy or unclean. This is how he introduced himself and assured them that he had no objection to complying with those who came for him; however, what he was really saying to them was that he no longer abides by the forbidden stipulation and did not see these people as unclean. So he asked them why they had sent for him.

Why was he here? Let's look back at John's account of Jesus's teaching on being the good Shepherd. He told them that He had other sheep of a different fold, and He must bring them in as well, so that they will also hear His voice, respond, and join their flock, becoming one with one Shepherd. (John 10:16) The other sheep He was speaking of are the gentiles, and Peter has arrived to bring them into the fold, unlocking the third and last door.

Cornelius answered him in two parts. He first shared that he had been praying when a man (angel) appeared to him and told him God had received his prayers and alms. He was to now send a party to Joppa, find Peter, and invite him to return with them. Part two was to hear his message from the Lord, the message the Lord was preparing for him.

Peter had previously delivered a similar message at Pentecost and in defense against the Sanhedrin. His opening remarks were well placed, as he assured them that God does not show partiality, but to all those everywhere who fear Him and do what is right, He gladly receives them. He then pointed out the keys they needed to hear:

1. Jesus is Lord of all.
2. Jesus's life and baptism by John.
3. The indwelling of the Holy Spirit.
4. His ministry.

5. His Crucifixion, by His own people.
6. His resurrection with proof through eyewitnesses, as the apostles saw Him eat and drink with them.
7. The great commission: to share the message that all who believe in Jesus Christ, and through faith in His name, the forgiveness of sin can be secured to have a right relationship with the Father.

Before Peter's next words, the Holy Spirit entered and took residence inside each of those joined together in that room, absorbing every word out of his mouth. I have searched the scriptures and many interpretations, and nowhere does it record that they took any action on their part to confess Christ and repent. Here is an open book where Christ, Himself, knew their hearts were full and prepared; therefore, He was ready to claim them for Himself by anointing them with His Spirit. Just as at Pentecost, they began to speak in tongues, supposedly Greek and Aramaic, so they would be understood. What a glorious sight as the Lord brought these gentiles into His church.

Speaking of awe in the room, the six witnesses Peter had brought with him (circumcised Jews) were amazed as they heard the Holy Spirit speaking through them in tongues. They were also in awe that the Lord would receive someone uncircumcised. This is something wonderful and glorious that they could no longer keep for themselves. The third and final people group has now been added to the church.

Peter spoke up and ordered them to be baptized in the name of Jesus to confirm their decision. His words validated their right to baptism by stating that they had received the Holy Spirit, just as He and others had. Now these new gentile believers were being joined in harmony with their Jewish and Samaritan brothers and sisters. You see, baptism is the evidence of being saved. First the Word is heard, then faith in Christ is realized, repentance takes place, the Holy Spirit moves in, and baptism affirms they are a new creature, a child of God.

Another stubborn crag has now been smoothed over, and this stone is being polished by the Lord, Who had faith in him knowing he was the one purposed to initiate the creation of His church, despite his flaws. We have flaws too; however, our Lord knows us and knows how He plans to use us if we will just allow Him to do so. As we have seen with Peter, Jesus had to walk him through the process of growing him to get to this point in his ministry, and an exclamation point it was. This was not the final crag, as we will soon see.

I would like to pause here and briefly look back at a pivotable point in Peter's walk. It was before Jesus ascended, when He had breakfast on the shore of Galilee with Peter and some of the apostles. Remember: Jesus took Peter aside and gave him three commissions: 1) tend my lambs, 2) shepherd my sheep, and 3) tend my sheep (John 21:15–17). What He was asking Peter to do is now realized and will continue until his death. The lambs are the young who make up the three people groups of the church Peter had witnessed to, taking them through the process of becoming the children of God. The sheep were the mature ones he had nurtured, taught, and discipled to care for those lambs (new believers). This once-craggy pebble is now becoming a smooth stone through clinging to the polisher and obeying His Words.

We have now visited Peter inserting the three keys that would unite the Jews, Samaritans, and gentiles. Three peoples who were enemies are now joined as one in Spirit. A nation that began when God chose twelve tribes would be changed by twelve apostles, serving the one true living God through the work of His Son, Jesus Christ.

Looking back, we find where one person stepped forward in each instance to reach many:

1. Pentecost. Jesus spoke with Peter twice, preparing him (Matthew 16:19; John 21:15–17). Peter then delivered the sermon at Pentecost that opened door #1, forming the church (just Jews at this time).
2. Philip, the evangelist, ventured into Samaria, where Jews would not go (Acts 8:5–12). They were a mixed breed and considered unclean. Philip preached the Gospel of Jesus Christ, healed, and performed miracles, bringing many to Christ; however, Peter and John would complete the process by instilling the Holy Spirit within them. Philip was that one person who led the way for Peter to insert key #2.
3. Cornelius, a Roman gentile, was moving away from Roman gods and idols, seeking to know the one true God of the Jews (Acts 10:12, 33–48). Peter was called to come and present the Gospel to not only him but his family, friends, and others. Thus, Cornelius was that one person the Lord would use to prepare the way for Peter to insert key #3 and bring the Gospel to the gentiles.

The Lord prepared a person in each instance to bring others to know Him. Peter was the one who fulfilled the Lord's purpose; however, it took that one person to begin the process. This is an example to us. We can share our faith with someone, not knowing who is hearing or how they are receiving it. That message will spread, and you can be that one person to initiate it, for God knows who will be going through that door your message has unlocked.

Chapter 7

Peter Opens Door #3

The First Gentiles become Disciples of Christ

(Acts 10)

Questions

Day One. The Other Side of the Door (Acts 10:1–8)

1. Who is the person featured in these verses, and what do they say about him? Define a centurion; who does he represent?

2. Using verses 2–3, what do you gather about the centurion's faith, and what was missing?

3. What was he doing in verse 3, and what transpired? Who did he address, and why?

4. What was the message given to him in verses 4–6? How did he respond? We receive messages from the Holy Spirit, as He seeks to direct our lives. How do you respond to them? Is there one you would like to share?

Day Two. Peter's Preparation (Acts 10:9–16)

1. What time frame elapsed between these two visions? Where was Peter?

2. What did Peter realize as he was praying? Do you think this interruption was directed by the Holy Spirit?

3. Now Peter has a vision; how did it relate to his interruption?

4. What did he see, and how did it point to what Peter believed from his Jewish faith?

5. Who spoke to him, and how did Peter reply? How many times was this action repeated? Looking closely; what does this experience tell you about Peter? What did he say in them that reminds you of the old Peter?

Day Three. After the Vision (Acts 10:17–23)

1. As Peter was sorting out the vision, how was he interrupted? What was their purpose?

2. What did the Holy Spirit say to Peter, and how did he respond?

3. How did the two visions (Peter and Cornelius) come together to serve God's purpose?

4. They wanted Peter to go and deliver a message (verse 22). What was that message, and how was it related to Peter's three visions?

5. In response, what did Peter do? Why do you think he took six men with him?

Day Four. Peter's Arrival (Acts 10:24–29)

1. When the entourage arrived after a two-day journey, who welcomed them, and how?

2. Reading in verse 26, what was Peter's response? What does this say to you about Peter? What does this say to you as a disciple of Christ?

3. Verse 28 gives the reason behind Peter's visions. What was it? Explain your answer.

Day Five. Peter Inserts His Key (Acts 10:33–48)

1. Who did Cornelius invite to hear Peter's message, according to verse 24? The audience was now ready for this remarkable message.

2. How did Peter open his message (verses 34–37)? How do you think they were responding to it?

3. Put verses 38–43 in your own words. What is his message meant for the others?

4. While delivering his message, he was interrupted. How? What did it have in common with Pentecost?

5. What was Peter's directive at this point, and what was the response of those who traveled with him? How do you think they received it?

6. In summary, Peter inserted key #3, and what did the door open? What can we learn from this event in our own lives, as the Holy Spirit heeds us to show our faith?

CHAPTER 8

Defense, Persecution, Deliverance

(Acts 11 and 12; Galatians 1:18–19)

Defense (Acts 11)

After spending some time with Cornelius and sharing Jesus with him, Peter left, and we now meet him back in Jerusalem to be met with a response from the circumcised Jewish Christians. They were those who still held close the Law of Moses and its legalism. Some were converted priests (Acts 6:7). Thus, you can see why they were struggling with the addition of the gentiles and the fact that they were not required to be circumcised Christians; however, the complaint they faced him with was one he struggled with, and that was fellowshipping and eating with these new believers. They were still divisive, even though the church was composed of all three people groups. All were to be the same with their individual cultural and religious rules set aside. This group would continue to be a thorn in the ministry of Paul and those setting up churches in Asia Minor.

Peter presented his declaration of defense by sharing his a) vision in Joppa with God addressing this issue with him, b) the Holy Spirit's directing him and falling upon the gentiles as He had done at Pentecost, and c) Jesus predicting the Baptism of the Holy Spirit given in Acts 11:16–17. These were powerful words that bound his defense.

There was no rebuttal from the accusers. Instead, they "glorified God" and responded that God had also given to the gentiles repentance leading to a new life (Acts 11:18). What a dynamic reply. This proves that God can and will work on our behalf when we are speaking up and defending Him. He is there with you to support your love for Him.

Persecution and Deliverance (Acts 12)

Sadly, the greeting Peter received from the Jews, who refused to accept the gentiles into the church because they did not adhere to their traditions, was only partially accepted. There were still those who chose to stand by the law.

Herod, the grandson of the Herod who called for the killing of all boy babies under two years old in Bethlehem to seek out and find Jesus, is now the king over Judah. He was 100 percent loyal to his Roman position and knew having a good relationship with the Jewish leaders was to his selfish advantage; therefore, he followed the way of his ancestors and hated the church built on Jesus. He seized James, the brother of John, who was close to Peter and fished with him when they found Jesus and became his disciples. He had him beheaded, making James the first of the twelve apostles to be martyred. This relates back to when James and John's mother asked Jesus for her two sons to sit on either side of Him in the kingdom. Jesus told her that she had no idea what she was asking. He then asked if they were willing to drink the cup He was about to drink, and they replied that they were able (Matthew 20:20–22).

The traditional Jews gave their approval. These were those not converted and had become hostile to the church, which fueled Herod's hatred. He enjoyed being in good standing with them, so he decided to attack them by going up the chain to the top, making Peter his prey, as he was the most notable of the apostles, especially in adding the gentiles to the church. What a prize to present to them.

Herod found Peter and had him arrested, with a perfect plan to bring him to trial just after the Passover, which was followed by a seven-day Feast of Unleavened Bread, possibly executing him as his gift to those he was trying to impress. As we have seen, this was not Peter's first time to be imprisoned for his faith but the third time. This time would be different, as the two other times gave him the opportunity to share the Gospel. Herod took extra precaution to keep this prisoner behind bars, as he was chained to two guards even while he slept and two more outside of the cell; however, Peter was able to sleep peacefully because he trusted his Lord. The evidence?

1. Prayers. The church was praying for him (verse 12).
2. Jesus's prophecy that he would live to be an old man and then martyred (John 21:18–19).
3. Obedience. When the angel appeared, he obeyed his instruction and followed him out of the prison.
4. This was Passover, when the Jews were celebrating being delivered from their enemy, and now Peter would experience his own Exodus through the actions of the prayers of his people, the church.

Once Peter was safe and out of the guards' reach, the angel, his work fulfilled, left him alone. Peter was assured that the angel was sent from the Lord to rescue him from Herod and what he had planned for the Jewish people. I would imagine he was still in a state of amazement as he decided where he would go. Peter evidently knew where the church was meeting, as they mostly met in private homes, and that would be at the home of Mary, John Mark's mother; thus, this is where he went to assure them that he had been miraculously delivered from an impending trial. He assuredly felt their prayers and wanted them to see them answered. Isn't it always an astounding revelation when we hear or see our prayers answered or feel the prayers of others lifting us up? This is a divine sensation that is never reduced to commonplace in a believer's life.

Prayer not only works miracles in the life of the one being prayed for, but also affirms the power of prayer to the one who reaches out to the Lord, expecting Him to hear and answer. Never, ever doubt the power of prayer or put it off when the Holy Spirit leads you to stop and pray. Believe me and, most of all, believe Him, for He has a purpose and a time. You are the vessel chosen to act upon the beautiful communication with the Lord. Here, once again, a fulfillment of scripture when Gamaliel confirmed "but if it is from God, you will not be able to stop these men; you will only find yourselves fighting against God"[41] (Acts 5:39 NIV).

He arrived at the gate, knocked, and spoke. A servant girl, Rhoda, answered. By her response, I assume she was also a Christian, as just hearing his voice excited her to the point where she forgot to let him in and ran to announce it to those gathered inside. They either did not believe her or were so taken aback that they thought his angel had come in his place, and that possibly he had already been Herod's victim. Looking at scripture, we see reference to these responses (Psalm 91:11; Hebrews 1:14).

It is comical to picture them trying to figure out who is at the door sounding like Peter, rather than just seeing the evidence. They must have been in a state of shock. Thankfully, Peter was persistent and knocked until they came, as a group, to see for themselves. What a blessed revelation.

Peter quieted their excitement and gave an account of what had transpired in the prison and the angelic deliverance. He then thanked them for their prayers that reached the Lord to send His personal deliverer. Afterwards, he asked them to make sure James (half-brother of Jesus) heard what had transpired, as he was the leader of the Jerusalem church. Then, after visiting with them for a time, he left; where he went, we do not know, but the scriptures do mention some other appearances, which we will look at in completing his journey for his and our Lord and Savior.

By the way, Herod had all sixteen guards killed. God was not through with him. What followed is both tragic and amusing. He decided to go down to Caesarea, a beautiful Roman resort, to flee from Jerusalem. Remember: this was also where Peter shared the Gospel with the gentiles and brought them into the church. Herod's vacation was cut short. Note that he was a proud man and delighted in the people who declared he was god. God refuses to share His glory and place with no one, so here is where He shows it as He sent an angel to kill him. Word has it that he suffered for five days before succumbing to death. God was not going to allow him to die quickly or quietly

---

[41] Barker, et al., *The NIV Study Bible*, 1656.

but to suffer for his pride and hatred toward His children. God will always be there for His people, for like Peter, all we must do is "ask Him in prayer." Prayer worked a miracle here to protect and save the church, and prayer will protect and save us today.

Speaking of today, let us also look at this event today and into the future. Paul, who will soon visit with Peter, shared with the Romans that by being justified by faith, we are also saved from the wrath of God through His Son, Jesus Christ (Romans 5:9). This message is one that speaks of God's response to people, like Herod, who despise those who cling to their faith in Jesus, now and in the future (tribulation). We have the assurance that our Lord is protecting us from the presence of sin now and going forward until the end times (1 Thessalonians 1:10; 5:9). Why? Because Jesus lives within us through the indwelling of the Holy Spirit that He graciously gave to us at salvation.

Peter Receives Paul into His Home (Galatians 1:18–19)

Paul gives a brief glimpse into his early ministry around three years after he had returned from his time in Arabia, where the Lord took him to be alone with after his encounter and transformation. He is now a new crusader for Jesus rather than a persecutor. Who did he seek out? He went to Jerusalem to see Peter. He was hungry to know all he could about his new faith and the church. This was a special time between the two of them, for he stayed with Peter for fifteen days. It would have been a blessing to hear what they shared with one another about their love and commitment to the Lord. They were both different and unique. He even mentions that he saw Jesus's brother, James. What a glorious time he had growing in the Lord through the experiences of these two great men who had been with Jesus. One a half-brother, who grew up with Jesus, and one, a Christian brother, chosen by Him and called the "rock."

What is your story about how you found Jesus? Where does He fit into your life? Are you devoted to Him? Do you hunger to know Him better, study His Word, and spend precious time calling out to Him in prayer, and most of all, do you make Him a part of your daily life, sharing Him with others?

These two men answered the call from the Lord. One Jew opened the door to the Jews, Samaritans, and gentiles, then went forward to witness to the Jews. The other Jew went to the gentiles; however, the message they shared was the same: the Gospel of Jesus Christ. The Lord has a purpose for all who seek to follow Him. They fulfilled theirs.

We will visit them together again in the mission field, where another of Peter's crags is smoothed over (not removed, for he would never become perfectly smooth, as that belongs only to our Lord and the Father). Then, in Acts 15, we will see Peter in action as a member of the Jerusalem Council.

Chapter 8

Defense, Persecution, Deliverance

(Acts 11–12)

Questions

Day One. Acts 11:1–18

1. Who were those who had learned of Peter's ministry to the gentiles?

2. What was their issue with the inclusion of the gentiles in the church that was predominantly Jews?

3. In summary, what did Peter share with them to make his point? How did they receive it? How does this relate to you where you are right now in your faith walk? Are you offended when new people come into the church from a different culture or way of life?

Day Two. Acts 12:1–5

1. Who is now king over Judah? What was his position regarding the apostles, and how did he show it?

2. Who supported his actions? What do you think their intentions were by supporting him?

3. Who did he now seek, and what action did he take? Why do you think he took excessive precautions?

4. What protection did Peter personally have?

Day Three. Acts 12:6–17

1. Looking back at Peter's previous imprisonments and freedom, how is this one alike and different? How did Peter react?

2. Two Jameses are mentioned, one in verse 2 and the other in verse 17. Who were they?

3. Connect the slain James with Matthew 20:20–22. What is Jesus prophesying to James's mother? This prophecy was fulfilled in only one part. Why could Jesus not assure her of the other? Why did their mother make this request?

4. Are you careful in making requests to the Lord in prayer? Are they humble requests or prideful ones? How do you think Jesus receives both?

5. When Peter arrived at Mary's house, what did those gathered think had happened to him?

Day Four. Acts 12:20–23

1. What happened to Herod, and why? See Isaiah 42:8 and 48:11. How do these scriptures apply here? What lesson is learned from this event?

CHAPTER 9

The Last Crag Smoothed by God's Appointed Apostle (Galatians 2:11–21), and the Jerusalem Council (Acts 15)

Here, we will find the remaining crag dealt with through the apostle Paul. Remember: Peter held the keys of authority over the church, given to him by Christ; however, Paul, the apostle chosen after Jesus's ascension, would hold the Sword of the Spirit that would confront and cut through the idols of the pagan religions throughout the known world, especially in Asia Minor and eastern Europe.

The gentile church was headquartered in Antioch (Syria), as the Jewish Christians were in Jerusalem under the watchful eyes of James and the other apostles. This scene opens in Antioch, where Peter was visiting and enjoying being with the gentile church, which also included Jewish believers. Reminiscent of his vision before going to the house of Cornelius, visiting there, and bringing the first gentiles into Christianity and the Lord's church, he was eating and fellowshipping with this blended church, who were one body and where former Jewish traditions did not separate them, for they were united in their faith of Jesus Christ.

All was joyous until company came calling. They were from the circumcision party, Jewish believers who claimed to have been sent by James; however, there is no proof of their accountability. Here is where that last stubborn crag will protrude, and the old Peter will show up, as he was fearful of them and felt threatened, thus appearing to not stand for what he had been preaching. Some might say he was acting like a hypocrite. His strong stance and appealing voice had faltered. He was returning to the ways of the law. He slowly withdrew and separated himself from affiliating with his gentile believers. His actions influenced the other local Jews, even Barnabas, who had accompanied Paul in support of the Antioch church. This is dangerous ground, as they had been professing, teaching, and fighting for unity in the church, a church that was built on faith in Jesus Christ and the Gospel of His death, resurrection, and ascension. He was the way, the only way of salvation. Circumcision was not necessary for justification, and God made no difference between whether a believer was Jew or gentile. Peter was separating the two by his actions. He was tearing down what he had been instrumental in putting together.

Paul publicly rebuked Peter by reminding him that he was a Jew but living as a gentile, so how could he expect the gentiles to live as Jews (Galatians 2:14)? He had every right to deliver this sharp accusation, for he was a Jew like Peter, who had turned his heart and ministry toward the gentiles. He made a point to those listening, especially Peter, when he asserted that he had died to the law, which we saw in the changed man he became after Jesus interrupted his trip to Damascus. A point was stressed that if a person held fast to the law and broke it, no justification could come through the works of the law because it is an act of God and not a process. The law was given to reveal our sins but could not redeem us from them. Redemption means "to pay a price for the release of someone." God sent His Son, Jesus Christ, to die on the cross as our sacrificial Lamb. Jesus paid the price to replace the law so all sinners who come to Him, confess their sins, repent, and ask Him to be their Savior are eternally His, being joined to Him forever with others from other places who have made that same confession. This is where Paul gives his personal testimony, removing the self-centered, legalistic person behind and becoming the Lord's apostle through the indwelling of the Holy Spirit.

His remarks continue through the remaining verses in the chapter, introducing the word *justified*, meaning "to declare righteous." He made a point that man does not receive justification by way of observing and participating in the law but strictly by faith in Jesus Christ alone.

Paul wraps up his discourse against Peter by pointing out that if righteousness came through the law, then Jesus died without purpose. God's grace gives people that for which they don't work. The Judaizers felt they could mix legalism and grace; therefore, he wanted them to know that they do not mix. As we say, oil and water do not mix. Peter was denying the grace God had granted to him at salvation, which he had preached to others. He was guilty of what Paul has just stated.

Peter's response is not given; however, we will see it played out through him at the Jerusalem Council. Please note that Paul's correction did not affect their relationship, as Peter called Paul a "beloved brother" in his second Epistle.

The Jerusalem Council (Acts 15:1–30)

This is the arena where the most important questions of doctrine are addressed and answered. Here is where any conflict regarding the doctrine of Jesus Christ and justification through faith in him was held fast and in no way mixed with or challenged by the law and the legalism attached to it. They were to stand firm in the fact that salvation is totally by the grace of God through His Son, Jesus Christ, and faith in only Him. It is in this setting where we last encounter Peter's life and ministry in God's Word, other than his two Epistles.

The main characters are James, who represents the elders, and Peter, the apostles. This meeting was the one that would either strengthen the church or divide it. What purpose brought this decisive meeting? Some Pharisees had become Jewish believers, yet they still held on to the Jewish belief that circumcision must be included in the salvation process. They became known as Judaizing Christians and held fast to the condition that the gentiles must adapt to this Jewish ritual and traveled around preaching it. Specifically, they had traveled to the church at Antioch to stress their belief, which caused a major issue within the church; therefore, Paul and Barnabas were sent to the Council to present their case. They did not go directly to their destination in Jerusalem but stopped over in Phoenicia and Samaria to share the conversion of the gentiles, bringing immense joy to them.

This truly encouraged their mission. Encouragement, to give someone confidence, hope, support, and strength, is a powerful word used in scripture to build us up, as shown in Romans 15:5, Philippians 2:1, Hebrews 6:18, and more. It is a word we should share with others out of love and caring for one another and in our prayer life. Encouragement boosts and reinforces us to move forward in the purpose God has chosen for us. It can also be a positive force to people fighting a battle within their lives. May we all be encouraged in the challenges that daily come before us.

Upon arrival, they presented their case, supporting the Gospel given to both Jew and gentile be the same, being the Gospel of Jesus Christ alone through faith with no attachments (yokes) added. After hearing their concerns, Peter addressed those present. He reminded them that God had chosen him to take the "word of the Gospel" to the gentiles and "believe." God then gave them the Holy Spirit, just as He also did to us. He made no distinction between Jew and gentile, as both received it by faith alone. Furthermore, Peter reminded them that neither they nor their fathers had kept the law. He ended his speech by stressing to them they believed their salvation was through the grace of Jesus in the same way they were. James then affirmed his message.

At the end of the meeting, the following conditions were sent back to Antioch so that unity could take place among both groups:

1. The gentiles would not be required to be circumcised.
2. They would avoid idolatry and immorality, being sins common to the gentiles before coming to Christ.
3. They were not to eat meats offered to idols. In their culture, animals were offered as a sacrifice to the idols and then put in the marketplace to sell for food.
4. Meats that had been strangled were not to be eaten, as well. Strangled animals would still have blood within them, whereby otherwise the blood would have been drained out of them.

These conditions were more for ethical and moral purposes. Since most churches met in homes, they ate together; thus, these dietary restrictions, agreeing not to eat what the Jews considered unclean, would dissuade division, and they could dine together in harmony. This is also a good reason for today, as we Christians live in a world with others who are not of our faith; therefore, when we are entertaining others, we should be sensitive to their beliefs. This is called respect, and respect can soften a relationship, possibly leading someone to Christ. Upon Paul and Barnabas's return, the decision was well received. In conclusion, this event in Peter's life was purposeful through his remembrance of opening the door of bringing the gentiles into God's church.

Peter's last crag has now been smoothed, and he will continue his mission in spreading the Gospel and authoring two Epistles (1 and 2 Peter). Although the Bible documents that Peter's wife traveled with him on his missionary journeys (1 Corinthians 9:5), tradition suggests she was crucified, Peter encouraging her to remember her Lord. Later, when his time came, he asked to be crucified upside down, as he was unworthy to die like his Lord. As I was reading this, I remembered an old movie, *Quo Vadis,* that was centered on Nero burning Rome and blaming the Christians, torturing and killing them, which included crucifixion. *Quo Vadis* is a Latin phrase meaning, "Where are you going?" Peter knew where he was going, and that was to be rejoined with his Master, who never turned His back or gave up on him. Jesus had put Peter's past in the darkness of night and his future in His glorious light. What a joyous reunion that must have been.

Where are you going? Are you going to allow your faith in Jesus to guide and direct your path? Faith is the evidence of things unseen, not what we can see. Are you willing to walk in faith and not fear, or do you need to see before you obey? If the patriarchs of the Bible had walked in fear, they would not have been the dynamic leaders God chose them to be. They would have never found the Promised Land or walked through the Red Sea. Will you allow your faith to be your eyes in sending you forward into the purposes the Lord has planned for you?

Chapter 9

The Last Crag Smoothed by God's Appointed Apostle (Galatians 2:11–21), and the Jerusalem Council (Acts 15)

Questions

Day One. Paul's Rebuke of Peter (Galatians 2:11–21)

1. What was the reason for Paul to rebuke Peter? From what you have learned about Peter up to this point, why do you think Paul took this action?

2. What affect did Peter's actions have upon the other Jewish Christians? What does this show you about how you conduct yourself around others?

3. Explain the difference of being justified by the law and justified by faith in Christ using Paul's illustration in verses 16–21?

Day Two. The Jerusalem Council (Acts 15:1–30)

1. Who were the Jerusalem Council, and for what purpose did Paul and Barnabas come before them (verses 1–2)?

2. Peter gave a speech in verses 7–11. What did he share about his ministry that directly connected to this situation? Who spoke up in verse 13, and what confirmation did he give per the prophets (verses 16–18)?

3. What was the decision they made, and what stipulations were attached to it? Why do you think it was important to include these? How can you apply this to your life?

TAKEAWAY FROM PETER'S LIFE AND MINISTRY

We have so much to learn about ourselves in the life of this great apostle. Each event in his life created a spoke in the wheel that moved the Gospel to the known world.

1. God doesn't call the equipped; he equips the called. That's you and me, as well. He takes us right where we are and begins to mold us to "be like Him" to fulfill His purpose for our lives. He knows our personalities, our frailties, our weaknesses, and our strengths. He also knows how He is going to use all of you to create that new creature. Such was the case of Peter, for Jesus took his old traits of being spontaneous, rambunctious, bold, and short-sighted to remold them into serving Him and serving Him well.

2. Peter never quit on the Lord. He picked up the pieces, learned from his mistakes, and never stopped going forward in bringing new souls into the kingdom.

3. Peter, at times, was weak. He denied the Lord, and he told the Lord no more than once when he refused to accept and eat the forbidden animals shown to him by the Lord. Did the Lord turn His back on him and choose another apostle? No, He hung in there with him all the way.

4. Peter was given three commissions in response to the three denials. The Lord did not even mention the denials. He met Peter right where he was, and the past was behind him. Jesus takes us right where we are and does not hold us accountable for our past; instead, He discards it.

5. Jesus was Peter's protection and rescued him numerous times, as he was miraculously rescued from each persecution. Peter remembered that Jesus had promised him a long life.

He trusted and believed Jesus's words. We can trust and believe that Jesus is always there for us through His Holy Spirit to watch over and care for us in tough times.

6. Peter required discipline, received it, and grew from it. He could have shunned Paul's rebuke, but his actions were checked by an appropriate person, this apostle of Jesus. Sometimes, our words and actions are not of the Lord's will, and we require discipline. It is not meant to harm us, but to encourage and strengthen us to make corrections and amends. I am thankful for these in my life, as sometimes they are things we cannot see alone.

7. The Lord put Peter in a notable position of leadership. Despite his crags, he was a great leader with a humble, serving spirit.

It is my hope that you are growing to be the person Jesus is molding you to be, someone who will project Him in all aspects of your life, both publicly and privately. Do your best, and let God do the rest.

BIBLIOGRAPHY

Barker, Kenneth, Donald Burdick, John Stek, Walter Wessel, and Ronald Youngblood, eds. *The NIV Study Bible.* Grand Rapids, MI: Zondervan Publishing House, 1995.

Brisco, Thomas V. *Holman Bible Atlas.* Nashville, Tennessee: B&H Publishing Group, 1998.

Brooks, James A. *The New American Commentary, Mark, Vol. 23.* Nashville, Tennessee: B&H Publishing Group, 1998.

Holy Christian Standard Bible. *Holy Bible, The Old & New Testaments,* Ultrathin Reference Edition. Nashville, Tennessee: Holman Bible Publishers, 2004.

Howley, G. C. D., F. F. Bruce, H. L. Ellison, eds. *The New Layman's Bible Commentary in One Volume.* Regency Reference Library. Grand Rapids, Michigan: Zondervan Publishing House, 1979.

Lawson, J. Gilchrist, ed. *The Christian Worker's New Testament and Psalms, Authorized King James Version.* Grand Rapids, Michigan: Zondervan Bible Publishers, 1981.

Lockyer, Herbert. *All the Apostles of the Bible.* Grand Rapids, Michigan: Zondervan Publishing House, 1972.

Macartney, Clarence Edward. *Peter and His Lord, Sermons on the Life of Peter.* Nashville, Tennessee: Abingdon Press, 1938.

Magee, J. Vernon. *Thru the Bible with J. Vernon Magee, Volume V, 1 Corinthians—Revelation.* Nashville, Tennessee: Thomas Nelson, 1983.

Robertson, A. T. *Epochs in the Life of Simon Peter.* Charles Scribner's Sons, 1935.

Ryrie, Charles Caldwell. *Ryrie Study Bible, Expanded Edition, New American Standard Bible.* Chicago: Moody Press, 1995.

Strassfeld, Michael. *The Jewish Holidays: A Guide and Commentary.* New York: William Morrow, 1985.

Strong, James. *Strong's Exhaustive Concordance of the Bible.* Nashville, Tennessee: Crusade Bible Publishers, Inc.

Walvoord, John F., and Roy B. Zuck. "The *Bible Knowledge Commentary, New Testament.* Colorado Springs: David C. Cook, 1983.

Wiersbe, Warren W. *The Wiersbe Bible Commentary, New Testament.* Colorado Springs: David C. Cook, 2007.